AGAINST MY FATHER'S WILL

A Memoir

Jane Morgan Barry

First Edition

ISBN (paperback): 978-0-578-56722-8
ISBN (ebook): 978-0-578-56723-5

Published by Back Shore Publishing
https://backshorepublishing.com

ACKNOWLEDGEMENTS

One doesn't write a book, much less publish it, without a lot of help and support. I would like to acknowledge my readers: Hedda Goodman, a quiet, wise woman, who read the book in its infancy and encouraged my writing of it from the very beginning; Eunice Gibson, former City Attorney in Madison, who not only offered guidance during the writing but was a moral support as I battled sexism in Maple Bluff. My high school cheerleading pal, Anne Craven Kipp, who taught English all her career, read the book in its early form and helped its development. Barbara Ligon, such a literate, luminous lady, a dear friend from long ago, also read the book in its infancy at least twice and provided me with copious, detailed comments. She, too, kept it alive because she validated the effort.

Then there are my Smith College alumnae friends: Nan Fitzpatrick, U.S. Senator, Tammy Baldwin, Elizabeth Tener and June Roberts, all of whom took time from their busy schedules to read the book and share their opinions and valuable guidance. Smith grad, Kirsten Kirby, publisher of her own book, *Your White Coat is Waiting: Vital Advice for Pre-Meds*, heard about my memoir, asked to read it, encouraged me to publish it and then offered to help me do that, 'gratis.' Since then, she has made it her business to see this book in print. For that I am eternally grateful. She has facilitated in all regards. Her creativity and technological skills have been critical. I think she's brilliant.

Mary Taborsky Varda, my 1968 Smith classmate, dear friend and native of Maple Bluff supported my activism even at risk to her own reputation in her childhood neighborhood and has encouraged my writing through the years. Finally, Carrie Baker, though not a Smith alumna, but rather Professor of the Study of Women and Gender at Smith, took time to advise me on this project.

I have had some professional editorial advice from Marion Sandmeier and Molly Schulman. They both helped a former academician, schooled in literary criticism, to develop the ability to bring the episodes herein to life by "showing" rather than "telling."

Finally, my family: My daughter, Margaret, forced me to search my feelings, touch my vulnerability, my culpability. Because of her I rewrote a lot of the book so that it isn't simply a story about external events but instead is a personal sharing of my emotional journey to become a full adult woman. The book now captures my internal struggles in an honest way that is much truer to who I am and what I've been through. She saw my story as an example of the universal struggle to affirm and love oneself—the external manifestations - my feminist battles and the tension with my father—simply as the particular media in which that quest occurred. Compelling me to touch that painful truth, that my journey has been to love myself, was Margaret's most precious contribution not only to the book but to me as a person.

My daughters, Lydia and Neville, have also been encouraging me through the years.

As I list all who have contributed to this book, I realize I have been blessed by a circle of women each of whom in her own way has supported my effort to share my journey from eternal daughterhood to affirmation of myself—a journey that continues to this day.

This circle includes my dear sister, Kathryn, for whom the book is not easy because it opens old wounds. She gently helped me acknowledge my too simplistic contention that I was disfavored in Dad's will only because my father was angered by my independence and activism. It is true that he didn't appreciate or approve of my feminist activities, but she rightly argued that the situation of the will was much more complex; that Dad loved both of us and our mother to the end; that his action in the will was an imperfect expression of that love. Her wisdom brought me to a deeper understanding that my personal feelings of guilt, my own doubts about my worthiness of the equality I sought, my own feelings that I deserved punishment for such presumption, may well have colored my perception of his act, projecting onto him the condemnation I levied against myself. I will never know for certain, but that is a possibility...and one that is comforting.

Dave, my husband: My eyes fill with tears when I think of our life together and his steadfast love. I was a cheerleader as a girl. Dave became my cheerleader in my womanhood. He has not only stood on the sidelines cheering me on as I battled the outside world, he has stood by me and cheered me on as I have battled within, searching for myself and my voice. Finally, he has insisted that my story is worth sharing.

We've always had dogs in our married life. Early on, when we were PhD students together and would walk hand in hand along Lakeland Avenue in Madison, WI, dreaming about our future, he would hold up our held hands and say "paw in paw" forever. He has honored that phrase. He has loved me enough to help me love myself. Thank you Dave.

Paris, le 06/07/2017 à bord du Cristal II

CHAPTER 1

The last of the mourners were making their way into the narthex for the service. We were still sitting in our rental car across the street and a few doors up the hill from the church. From there I could recognize many of the parishioners, though faded and less erect now. I remembered them full of vigor, laughter, energy as they attended our wedding in 1968 and peopled my sunny childhood. I could see Herb Macleod, the tall, bald Scotsman, who would leave his blue-collar job every Friday afternoon only to dedicate his weekends to the upkeep of the church. He had assumed his customary Sunday post at the church door wearing a tartan tie for the occasion. It was his way of honoring the memory of Mom who always brimmed with pride about her own Scottish heritage. Like most of the members of the church—my parents among them—he was an honorable man who had worked hard for a modest living. "Decent" was the word Mom always used to describe the people of Park Avenue Congregational Church. While its name conjured up *the* Park Avenue, this was Park Avenue in Arlington, Massachusetts. Most here came into the world with nothing more than their dreams, eked out an honest, hard living for their families, only to pass quietly on, leaving behind little more than their children and the modest homes they spent their lives struggling to purchase and conscientiously, lovingly tending.

That congregation—those people—were the stock from whence I came. On both sides of my family, my grandparents, like my parents, worked hard. Both grandfathers rose to be foremen in factories. Both grandmothers raised the children and did all the domestic chores with none of the luxuries or help I have had.

While I recognized and fondly remembered many of the parishioners,

1

cherishing the past and my parents whom they represented, I didn't want to meet and talk with them at that moment. I felt uncomfortable, certain that if they knew of the rift between my family and me, their sympathies would lie with "Kathryn", my sister Kathryn, who had stayed in Arlington all her life and remained a faithful member of the church—not with me, who after 25 years in Wisconsin had become an outsider if not a stranger.

I was there now because I couldn't not be. I couldn't allow my mother to be buried without saying "Good Bye" and "I love you" one last time, without expressing my respect by my presence. Everything in me wanted to be there. Yet, it wasn't easy. Too much had happened since I made that terrible choice.

I had returned because despite everything, I loved and still love my mother.

I knew that Kathryn and her family—her husband, Peter, and their two sons—would be sitting in the proper place for "the family," the front of the church near our mother's casket. I couldn't miss the funeral, but I couldn't be there in the family pew with Kathryn either. If I sat beside her as if nothing were wrong between us, I would in effect, be condoning my parents' actions as she seemed to have done. That was the last thing I wanted to do.

As I approached the church door, Herb, whom I hadn't seen for many years, greeted me familiarly and gently with sad eyes. If he knew of the rift, he wasn't taking sides—at least not this morning:

"Janie," (everyone from my childhood still called me Janie despite my discomfort with its implication of childishness). "It's good to see you. Sad about your Mom." Squeezing back tears, cheeks quivering, I nodded to thank him for his kind words, and silently took the "Order of Worship" from him.

There in black and white on cheap, flimsy paper, the Order of Worship this morning was "In Celebration of the Life of Margaret ('Peg') McCall," my mother. So simple, so stark, so undeniable, so final.

The sanctuary was fittingly subdued, even gloomy. The wood trim and exposed brick walls, bright, new and modern in the 1960's when Dad was on the Building Committee, when Mom helped raise money organizing "The Black Cat Fair" every October and when I was just a teenager, had aged, like us, over the thirty years. The gasoline fumes from all the cars on the busy street outside, the perspiration of the parishioners in the pews on sultry, summer mornings had sullied the once shiny, new church. Now, virtually unnoticed in the gloom, Dave and I quietly took seats at the rear of the half-filled church, next to Di, my dear childhood friend, who was waiting for us.

This was the church my mother attended for 60 of her 73 years; the church in which she and my father were married; the church in which my sister and I were baptized and confirmed; the church in which David and I were married—and the church of my father's funeral four years prior.

I, the first-born child, once the "golden girl," "the apple of your father's eye" as Mom so often had said, was sitting in the rear-most pew at my own mother's funeral. I felt irreverent and errant for my absence from the front pew—and for my absence from the wake the previous night—but I couldn't pretend that everything was just fine when it wasn't.

There Kathryn was up front, but I could only see the back of her head. When Kathryn was a kid, Mom had always commented on its immense size. It seemed so because she was such a skinny little thing, with spindles for legs. Now, it seemed strangely small because of the distance between us. Her husband, their two sons, my nephews, my Auntie May and Uncle Warren, their two sons, my cousins, and their families were up there with my sister. Kathryn was sitting directly in front of the casket in the first pew surrounded by supportive family members—where daughters are supposed to be. The casket bearing my mother was just feet from her. I could see it way up at the head of the sanctuary in front of the altar. My physical distance, a metaphor for the fracture in our relationship, now

3

made the whole thing feel less real—more difficult to conceive that my mother was dead in that box. I silently said: "Mom, I am here."

My husband, Dave, was on one side of me on the plain, modern pew. He reached out and took my hand, always my loving support. Di, my best friend since fourth grade, was on my other side. The rest of the congregation stretched before us separating me from my family, from my mother. It was 10:00 on Tuesday morning, May 12, 1997. Mom had died unexpectedly, that past Saturday night minutes before Mother's Day.

Suddenly, the organ burst forth with a familiar hymn, "Holy, Holy, Holy, Lord God Almighty." I sang fervently. I could hear my mother's reedy, pretty voice singing beside me. We'd sung this hymn hundreds of times together. I always felt inspired by it. Now, I was communing with her spirit—and with the strong sense of Christian community, stability, and tradition, to which she and my family belonged. I'd been away a long time. I had questioned the legitimacy of the belief, but some things are so deeply rooted, time and intellectual considerations have no effect.

But she wasn't here anymore. She was dead in that casket. Gone forever. The muscles in my throat were tightening, my cheeks shivered, a hot tear quietly inched its way down my face. I felt isolated.

As the music stopped, a minister stepped forward to give the eulogy. I didn't recognize him. He was a stranger to me, an interim pastor. The regular minister was on sabbatical. After all the years that my mother attended and supported this church, a stranger, someone who didn't even really know her and certainly never knew her when she was well, was performing her burial service. My mother would be hurt and embarrassed by this. She valued relationships. She considered them her strength. She sacrificed her wishes, her desires, herself, for them. Despite the strain that had existed in our relationship, I was hurt for her, hurt on her behalf. I felt that she had been disrespected, or at least not respected enough for her minister to return to celebrate and bury her.

Significantly, the strange minister read passages from Proverbs defining "the virtuous woman"—the good wife: "Who can find a virtuous woman? For her price is far above rubies. The heart of her husband does safely trust in her, for that he shall have no need of spoil. She will do him good and not evil all the days of her life....Her husband is known in the gates, when he sits among the Elders of the land....She looks well to the ways of her household and eats not the bread of idleness."

Ironically, despite his strangeness to us, perhaps because of it, he hit a raw nerve. I loved my mother, but I never liked the role of "the virtuous wife" that she played, her significance defined primarily by how her behavior enhanced or detracted from her husband's reputation and well-being. Her commitment to this ethos had ultimately contributed to my estrangement from her. Fortunately, before her death we made our peace.

*

It was a Monday afternoon in March of 1994. On my way home to Madison from a National Alumnae Admissions Board meeting at Smith College in western Massachusetts, I dropped in unannounced to visit my mother at a Senior Center she attended. I arrived that day by 2 o'clock. Auntie May, Mom's only sibling, had told me that my mother was attending a different program now that her disease had progressed. Finding the place had been a race against time. I wanted to see Mom but I wanted to avoid seeing Kathryn with whom she now lived. I knew the program she attended ended mid-afternoon, but no one at the local town hall seemed to know exactly where it was held. When I finally arrived, I saw the bus that would transport my mother back to Kathryn's home already parked in front of the building.

As I hurried past it on my way to the building's entrance, something made me turn—perhaps to check my appearance so that I might pass inspection? I peered into the translucent window of the bus and as if in a mirror I saw a face a few inches from my own—but not my own: my

5

mother's. She was sitting there all alone—the only one in the bus—staring out the very window into which I looked. The remains of her makeup faded, no sparkle to her dark brown eyes, she was gazing in a distracted, unfocused way, at 72 only a shadow of the animated, dynamic person she had always been.

Startled by my presence, suddenly, recognition replaced her vacant gaze. She came alive smiling expectantly like a delighted child who suddenly spots her own mother arriving to pick her up at school. Vigorously signaling me to go to the front of the bus, we hurried in tandem, I on the outside, she on the inside, still straining not to lose sight of the other, until we both reached the open door and came face-to-face.

Standing on the top stair, smiling, she was the social hostess 'par excellence,' inviting a guest into her home. She gestured graciously toward the orange, molded plastic benches inside the chartered bus: "Come on in and sit down with me, why don't you...?" *Was it the disease? Was she assuming a familiar role to hide confusion?*

I could hear her admonitions of old—lessons passed on to me from her Scottish mother, my Grandmother Jean, for whom I was named: "You never invite someone into your home without offering them a bite to eat, Janie, even if all you have is a cup of tea. It's rude not to offer a guest something."

There was no tea anymore. She could not have made it if she had it. Now, all she had was the bus for a sitting room. But Alzheimer's never erased her sense of decorum. She was ever a lady despite her lowly economic station—and now even in her cruel demise.

Kathryn had seen to it that our mother looked dignified, dressed in a neatly pressed pair of heather gray slacks and a snug, red, boiled-wool jacket. From the neck down, she looked like a mannequin out of the Casual Corner window.

Responding to her invitation, I went up the stairs to the landing smiling and saying "Hi, Mom...."

I could say no more. The sparkle returned to her eyes. Her spontaneous joy at seeing me again—whether she knew that I was her first born or not—overwhelmed me. After the years of tension and distance, her uncensored, open expression of affection was a blessed relief, but I was overcome by a sense of loss.

What had become of Mom? Emotion trapped the words in my throat. I reached out, hugged her and we both sobbed. Her once lush hair felt dry and lifeless against my cheek, her once youthful, strong, vibrant body now small and frail as it shuddered with emotion. There were no complications now. Neither one of us was capable of that any more. I was still precious to her—as she was to me.

I had visited her twice and called frequently in the months since I learned of her illness, but I had to do most, and gradually all, of the talking. The disease robbed this once gregarious, woman of her ability to converse. Our meetings had been frustrating for me. She would smile, but that was the extent of her expression of emotion.

Now for the first time in years—and for the last time ever—we showed our love for one another the only way possible—through an embrace and tears. After all the distance and disappointment, we were standing on the stairwell of a public bus, clinging to one and other and crying.

That was the last time I ever saw my mother. She died unexpectedly of a stroke two months later when I was back in Wisconsin—mercifully before the disease robbed her of the last shred of herself—or of the "virtuous wife" she aspired to be.

*

The minister droned on, finally ending the passage: "Many daughters have done virtuously but you excel them all. / Favor is deceitful and beauty is vain but a woman who fears the Lord, she shall be praised...." Mom lived her life and taught us not to be "conceited." I understood that to mean that we shouldn't think of ourselves as important; shouldn't be

7

self-centered, self-loving, egotistical—or at least not show it. Instead we were to be humble...to fear and obey "the Lord," not just God, Himself, but all authority, all lords. Authority was not ourselves.

I was filled with sadness, rage, and frustration. This man was praising my mother for the very characteristics which estranged us, for the very lifestyle which fostered all the pretense. As a teenager, I had discovered my mother's facade. As an adult, I had condemned her for pretending inferiority to my Dad when I knew she was at least his equal, and really wanted to be more powerful and assertive of her own will. I distanced myself from her example. I have considered her a hypocrite. I raged at society's demand that she live a fiction, which encouraged—if not actually required—denial or subordination of her own desires, abilities and dreams. I grieved that she never achieved what she wanted. Her opportunity is gone forever.

I struggled with the separation between the image and the real woman. *Which was I mourning? Was I mourning the woman she appeared to be or the one she never really expressed?* I was mourning the amalgam and the fact that there *was* an amalgam, but I also clung to the bits and pieces of the person I know she was—but never became. She was ambitious but acted indifferent to wealth and prestige. Embarrassed, she hid her disappointment that Dad never "made it" under the cover of Christian indifference to worldly gains. "Money and material goods are not what's important in life...."

They may not be all there is, or even the most important part of life, but she wanted more worldly gains than she got. She was smart, but never developed her mind. Women didn't do that, especially if her husband might have been eclipsed. She loved her children, but her duty to enhance her husband's image, his standing in the family and the community, ultimately superseded all emotional attachments—even to me, her first-born, the projection of all her hopes and dreams.

After the funeral Dave and I headed to Manomet—a town just south of Plymouth on the way to Cape Cod—and to the cottage where I spent every summer of my childhood. With Mom's death and my situation with Kathryn at a stalemate, I thought this might be the last time I'd be at this place where my family was so happy together. I wanted to say goodbye.

The cottage was the place where I could best reconnect with the memory of Mom. I think she was happiest there, wearing a faded bathing suit and one of Dad's old sailor hats from World War II. At Manomet there were fewer expectations, the need for fewer pretensions. She loved the sun and the smell of the sea. Every time we arrived at the cottage, she would challenge us: "Can't you just *smell* that salt air?" She'd wait for us to assure her we could: "Yes, Mom, we can smell it!" Then inevitably she'd close her eyes, pucker her nose and shaking her head from side to side, she'd say: "Umm...I just *love* that smell!" And she did.

Driving up the bumpy, unpaved hill I caught sight of the little mint green, painted Cape Cod house dwarfed by the gigantic rhododendron bush Dad had planted for mom back in the '50's. It was all so familiar and comforting, reminiscent of hundreds of other arrivals in happier times. "Manomet"—we'd always called the cottage by the name of the town—Manomet had always been a happy place. Days spent eating our picnic lunches on the beach, the ever-present baloney and cheese mixed with sand, cherry or grape flavored Zar-X drink mixed with sand, Oreo cookies mixed with sand, and playing on the gigantic rocks along the shore. Those rocks were a constant source of frustration for my mother, who wanted the beach to be sandy and smooth like the beach at West Harwich where her good friends from Park Avenue Church, Charlotte and Bill, had their summer cottage. I guess to the extent that Arlington impinged on Manomet, Mom did still occasionally feel the demands of expectations. But for us kids, the centuries had strewn the rocks there on the sand for our endless entertainment. At low tide, we'd jump from one to the other, pretending they were our homes, castles, or whatever, and lie on their solar heated surfaces to sunbathe after our exertion in the cold Atlantic. At high tide like sleek seals we'd swim between them, dive off, pull mussels from their sides for nighttime fish boils.

There were all the nights that our little cottage would reverberate with the strains of Scottish tunes like "You take the high road, And I'll take the low road, And I'll be in Scotland before ye" or American favorites like "Daisy, Daisy, Give Me Your Answer True" or "Take Me Out to The Ball Game." On those magical nights, Dad would emerge from the cramped closet in my parents' bedroom carrying the dusty, black suitcase containing the accordion he had learned to play in high school. Kathryn and I would squeal with anticipation of another lively evening of song and dance. It wasn't long after the music began that Mom couldn't resist the urge. Always slim and energetic, she'd twirl around the small living room in her Bermuda shorts, encouraging us girls—or the neighbors who often appeared in response to the wafting accordion strains—to join her. Every songfest ended the same way. Dad would smile at Mom and then play "Peg of my Heart.... I love you." Then everyone would join in for "Good Night Ladies/ Good Night Gentlemen."

I'd known Manomet for as long as I had lived on this planet. There had never been a time in my memory when Manomet was not in my life, never a summer when I couldn't count on my mother faithfully planting her pink, white and velvet purple petunias in the wooden window boxes my father had made with such painstaking care. They built the place for us together.

When we approached the home after the funeral, however, it looked sad. The shades were down at the living room windows; the lights were shut off; the window boxes empty, filled only with desiccated, gray soil; the paint around the windows flaking. Still, I wanted to be there. Dave and I pulled into the driveway and heard the crunch of the dead pine needles covering the parking spot where Dad had always parked his car, and we got out to look around. The sun was shining bright and warm. The air smelled of baking pine needles and the fragrance of the sea was strong as though waiting for Mom's appreciative sniff. The rhododendron, Mom's "Rhodie," was in full, pink bloom. It was just the kind of day she would have loved.

I went to the living room window to peer in through the small opening at the bottom of the shade. I couldn't see much—*but what is that?!* Shards of broken porcelain and what appeared to be slivers of wood were on the floor. My mind flashed back forty years. I had seen a similar sight then. *It's those damn squirrels again!* With all the shades down, I couldn't see much more. My imagination was racing. *Have they shredded the upholstery? Is the cottage destroyed?*

"May I help you?" The deep, querulous voice startled me. The question came from a stranger, acting indignant and proprietary, hovering behind me in our driveway.

"Who are *you*?" I asked—irritated by his accusatory, suspicious tone.

"I live next door,"—he was pointing at Ed and Mavis Lee's cottage which he must have bought, "I keep an eye on this place for the owner. My name's John Whiting."

"My name is Jane *McCall* Barry. I am Ron and Peg's older daughter."

I wondered if he knew about my estrangement. I looked for some indication. None. Mom and Dad were private people. True to form, they didn't seem to have shared their "dirty laundry".

"Oh! Nice to meet you, Jane! I've heard all about you."

What has he heard?

"You're the daughter who lives in Wisconsin! You look a lot like your sister, Kathryn!" Then he frowned: "I'm sorry about your mother's death. But you, of course, know that she was getting very sick. She'd wander around here all the time, confused. We were worried she'd get lost or hurt."

"Thanks for your kind concern, John.... We buried Mom today. I came here to reminisce, to commune with my memories of Mom and

11

Dad, but it seems that something bad has been going on in the house here. Do you know anything about it?"

Startled by that news, he practically shrieked: "No! What do you mean?!"

"Well, there's a mess on the living room floor. I know Mom and Kathryn would never have left it like that. I think squirrels may have gotten in."

"Oh dear! I had no idea!" he confessed, worried that the house may have been damaged under his watch.

I paused and decided to be forthright: "John, I'm in an awkward position, here. As I said, Mom was buried this morning and I've come today to commune with memories of my childhood, but I don't have any way of getting into the house to assess or solve the problem. My sister has the keys and I don't know if you are aware, but we are estranged."

"No! I...I didn't know that, but your mother and father probably wouldn't have confided that kind of information to me anyway...we were just neighbors."

Brightening, he said: "I have the keys to the house!" Then almost immediately, a look of concern came over him. "Oh, but...I'm sorry. I don't have permission to give them out to anyone...." He seemed a little uneasy and embarrassed to be included in a family secret and then to have to treat me like a stranger.

"Perhaps you would call my sister to let her know something's happened to the cottage?"

"Oh, of course! I...I'd be glad to." With that, he took the opportunity to escape. "I'll go do that right now. It was nice to meet you, Jane. Feel free to look around...."

The cottage—our cottage, my cottage—a place that held such happy memories, that held my past, was endangered. And I was anguished. I wanted to fix it—NOW. But I had no way to get in; I really didn't even have a right to be there anymore.

After all these years, after holding the boards on the wooden "horse" when I was a child so Dad could saw them straight to build the walls of our cottage, I was a trespasser in my own childhood home. A perfect stranger, some fellow named "John Whiting," was allowing me limited access: "Feel free to look around..." he said.

As Kathryn had often said: "Jane, you always do what you damn well please."

There was a price.

CHAPTER 2

In some sense my separation from my family, so painfully felt in the church at Mom's funeral in 1997 and at Manomet after Mom's funeral, started thirty-two years earlier in the same church.

David Barry appeared there that Sunday morning in 1965 to hear his former college roommate, our assistant minister, preach. As fate would have it, my mother was the greeter that day and I was home from college for spring break. Mom spotted Dave immediately as a hitherto undetected and eligible bachelor. There wasn't much at the Park Avenue Congregational Church in Arlington, Massachusetts that escaped Mom's notice.

I hadn't seen him in the congregation during the service because I had been singing in the choir. By the time my mother identified him as "attractive," I had long since stripped off my choir robe and sprinted headlong for the family car to await impatiently our departure for home. I was anxious. I had spent my whole spring break in Nassau with my Smith College housemates, socializing with lots of men from other colleges. It had been fun, but now reality imposed itself. I had mountains of reading and writing to do for the upcoming week's classes, none of which I had even begun. My stomach churned. I was terrified that I wouldn't be able to accomplish my assignments due the next day.

On greeting Dave, Mom dispatched Kathryn, to retrieve me for introductions. Breathless, having run up the hill to find me before the moment was lost, my sister, a young 15, announced with an excitement tinged with urgency: "Jane. You've got to come back to the narthex! Mom has a real nice guy she wants you to meet. Hurry! Hurry before he leaves!"

Exasperated, I grumbled: "I don't want to meet a 'real nice guy.' I just want to go home! I've got lots of work to do!"

15

Mom had prevailed upon me that morning to sing in the choir: "People will want to see you, Jane."—and sing, I had—but now I needed to get on with my life.·

Kathryn persisted: "Jane, Mom wants you to meet him. Come on!"

It was futile to resist. I had to comply. My parents were good to me. I owed them respect. They had brought us up to be obedient and I was nothing if not that. The McCall girls were exemplary "good girls." With a sigh I reluctantly complied.

When I got to the church door, I could see my mother's animation, her hands were gesturing, a smile on her face as she talked to this tall fellow with his back to me as I stood in the entrance. Mom was definitely engaged. All I could see of him other than that he was about 6 feet tall with a nice physique in his formal dark suit, was that he had an emerging bald spot in the back of his head. *Too old for me,* I thought.

At that moment, Mom spotted me: "Jane, come over here! I have this nice fellow to introduce to you." She was beaming, her dark brown eyes sparkling and her trim figure vibrant with excitement.

The fellow turned my way revealing classically balanced, tanned facial features framed by horn rimmed glasses. He was pleasant enough looking, but a lot more mature in appearance than the guys I socialized with in Nassau, and not drop-dead handsome, which might have balanced the age factor. Instead he looked very intellectual. I was only 19. I looked my age, neither older nor younger. I felt attractive. Many said I was beautiful. My hair was my most noticeable asset: long, lustrous, chestnut colored with natural auburn highlights and light blonde streaks from the sun. Five feet six inches tall, I was slim with a subtle figure. I seemed poised enough amongst my peers, but I was emotionally young: innocent, immature—in retrospect, retarded sexually. It wasn't long before my meeting Dave that Sunday, that I was in my high school boyfriend's car outside my parents' house after a date. We were kissing when my hand happened on an object in his lap. I was startled, totally oblivious of what

16

I had touched. He laughed. I was bewildered, then scared, and finally, humiliated by my own ignorance.

"Jane, this is David Barry. He's a friend of Rip Noble's from Princeton."

I knew Rip, but only as "Mr. Noble," the new Assistant Minister at my church. He and his wife were a nice, young, married couple but again, not *that* young! I considered them "adults," and myself not yet an adult...a hybrid between teenager and adult.

Mom continued proudly: "Jane goes to Smith College, David. She's heading back to Northampton later today. She's just back from Spring Break in Nassau with her college friends."

In this sound bite I seemed so successful: a Smith College student, having spent her vacation in the Bahamas with college friends. La dee dah!

She continued: "Jane, Dave went to Princeton. He's currently studying at Harvard Divinity School."

I smiled perfunctorily and nodded. *This introduction is useless. He's too old, mature and sophisticated for me and I certainly don't want to date a present or future minister! Doesn't Mom realize this? What is she thinking?*

"Hi, Dave, nice to meet you," I said.

"You go to Smith, huh?" he queried, giving me his undivided attention.

To me he felt like a friend of my parents asking me about my college, instead of a potential suitor.

"Yes, I'm a freshman there," I confirmed, hoping that he would realize I was too young for him.

But he continued to chat: "My sister is a Smithie, too. I know she loved it there. It's a great school!"

His interest in me was apparently enhanced by my college affiliation though my very best, sophisticated, raspberry colored, Virgin wool suit may have had its own effect. The suit was a Christmas present and I was very proud of it; it was the first really nicely tailored suit I'd ever owned and a brand worn by many of the prep school girls at Smith. It had a detailed, notched round collar with slit pockets on the fitted bodice. Under the jacket I had a soft pink, sleeveless, silk "shell," embellished with my initials, JMB, in raspberry colored thread. In it I looked a lot more affluent than I was. Dad worked many hours to pay for that suit. And little did this David Barry know, not only did I have no money, but also, I was barely hanging on at Smith!

I'm an all-round fraud!, I thought.

*

I went to Smith aspiring to fit in but it seemed my classmates were much smarter...or at the least, much better prepared than I. I couldn't keep up with the reading, the volumes that were expected of me each and every week. I didn't know how long I could last there. Mom and Dad were so proud of me, thinking I had made it. I wanted to be able to make the grade and realize their ambitions for me, but more and more I just didn't think I could.

When I applied at Smith what really caught my attention was how it—along with the other Seven Sister colleges—seemed the female alternative to the men's "Ivy League" which in those days was still adhering to their 200-year-old tradition of excluding all females on the grounds that they were intellectually inferior by nature. Despite the fact that I had taken every "male" course in high school and done well, I had become aware that I was ineligible even to apply to Harvard, Yale, Princeton, "the Ivies," because of my gender. I don't know that I consciously recognized the discrimination, but I do know that I was immediately entranced by the idea of the Seven Sisters Colleges when my mother informed me of their existence. It seemed that I would be applying to a college with a pedigree similar to that of the Ivies. Smith even featured an "Ivy Chain" graduation weekend composed of the seniors, each clad in a white gown and carrying a chain of real ivy over their left shoulder as they paraded through the campus the day before commencement.

There were other women's colleges, like Pine Manor Junior College, Bradford Junior College, Katie Gibbs, Goucher, Skidmore, Connecticut College, where a girl like me from the working-class world could surround herself with relative luxury and social prestige, but Smith, like the rest of the Seven Sisters (Radcliffe, Wellesley, Barnard, Mt. Holyoke, Vassar and Bryn Mawr) was special. With its antique oriental carpets everywhere, the Friday afternoon tea poured from ornate silver teapots, the Yale and Dartmouth men and the boarding school backgrounds of many of its students, Smith conferred social status, yes, but it also conferred equal intellectual status by its competitive admission policy. It offered the same, challenging, superior education available to men at the Ivies. At Smith, women were encouraged to concentrate on their own intellectual and professional development. There was no social stigma to being smart and accomplished. Like our college president's mother, a Smith alumna herself, (in those days, Smith's presidents were, of course, always men) who subsequently broke the gender barrier at Johns Hopkins Medical School to become one of its first female graduates, we were being educated not just to raise the next generation with more culture, but to remain active and influential in the public sphere in our own right.

My high school guidance counselor was encouraging when I expressed interest in applying to Smith. When I brought the hard facts about room, board and tuition costs home to my parents, Dad and Mom looked at the numbers:

"So, your guidance counselor thinks that you could get in here, Janie?"

"Yes, Mom. She thinks that with my SAT scores and my extracurricular activities, I would have a good chance. She also said that if we would need a scholarship, I should apply Early Decision. That way if I get in Early Decision but with no money, I will have a better chance to get scholarship money at Regular Decision since I will have demonstrated my sincere desire to go the school."

Dad was quiet, silently perusing the information. I looked at him to gauge his feelings. His expression was serious and tense.

Finally, he spoke: "Well, Jane, this place is really very expensive. Much more money than we can afford. That's for sure. You certainly would have to get a scholarship to go there. I mean $2,000 every year for four years. That's $8,000!"

Dad was distressed. I sensed that he would rather not have to deal with Smith, a place that he felt he couldn't afford.

Mom, on the other hand, seemed intrigued and excited: "Ron, I agree that it's more than we can handle, but there's no harm in Jane's applying to see whether she can get in, and if so, what they will give her for financial aid."

I knew that Mom wanted this for me and Dad acquiesced to the trial balloon. So, in the fall of 1963 I applied Early Decision to Smith College. By December, I was accepted but without any scholarship money. When in the following spring I received a substantial, but partial, scholarship, the decision had to be made whether or not the scholarship was enough. While I was exhilarated by all the possibilities that Smith promised, intellectual as well as social, my parents were mightily conflicted.

While Dad was negative, Mom was enticed by the prospect that her daughter would matriculate at such an elite, private college. She was proud of my academic accomplishment and thrilled at the social prestige she thought my association with the place would confer on our family.

She excitedly greeted me one day right after my Smith acceptance, with a letter that had arrived while I was at school: "Jane, look what came in the mail today! This is from Patience Hosmer, my cousin, Charlie MacPherson's wife. You know. I've told you about Charlie. He went to Harvard and married a girl from Smith who is from a very prominent, old, blue-blood family in Concord? They live in Acton now. Remember?" She was almost hyperventilating.

I did remember hearing about them from Mom, but had never actually met them: "Do you know her, Mom?"

"Mmm no, uh.... I...I've never...met her," a cloud forming over her face, then her eyes brightening, she blurted, "But when we were kids, Charlie and I were very close!" She paused with a wistful, distant look as she seemed to envision that time long ago: "I've lost touch with Charlie over the years...."

Concord and Acton were only a few miles apart, and only 15 minutes' drive from Arlington, but they were in a different orbit. Cousin Charlie had left my mother's world when he went to Harvard and married a blue-blood. Now he and his wife traveled in very different circles from my parents and their friends at Park Avenue Congregational Church. Through the Smith Alumnae network "Patty" had discovered that I had been accepted at Smith so she had written a gracious, welcoming letter on engraved, monogrammed stationery to me and my parents. The letter appeared in our mailbox like an invitation to a royal wedding, with a hand script and heavy, textured paper different from all the usual letters in our box. Mom was proud and excited to have communication from the fancy side of the family.

Dad was the real obstacle. He took pride in paying his way. He couldn't afford the tuition at Smith without scholarship or loan help.

In April of my senior year in high school, 1964, we were on the Smith campus for a final deciding tour. The apple blossoms, daffodils, tulips were all in bloom. The place was like Paradise. In fact, the pond we were walking by was called Paradise Pond. Even though I had received scholarship money, the deficit was still $800/year, a lot of money for my Dad to pay as the sole bread-winner, a draftsman at a manufacturing plant in Cambridge.

The choice was momentous: *would I be allowed to matriculate at this prestigious college which afforded entree into a forbidden, elite world or would I have to settle for a state school which my parents could more*

21

comfortably afford and where I would stay in my native milieu? As we walked around the campus and discussed the decision, I could tell that my mother was still enthusiastic, beguiled by the beauty, delighted by the prospect of a daughter at Smith. She had always had social aspirations herself; she may have been a WASP (a white Anglo-Saxon Protestant), but she had no money and no lineage of power. Even if she had shown academic promise as her sister, my Aunt May, had, there was no money to pay for an education beyond high school. If I, her daughter, went to Smith, by association she too would rise socially. To her, that had great appeal.

Dad continued his resistance, though: "Jane, there is no doubt that this is a beautiful place and I'm sure the education is excellent, but this is really beyond our means. Why can't you just go to UMass (*down the road a piece and a world away*) and get a good education that we can afford? You might go here and feel bad because you don't have the right clothes to wear or enough spending money."

Dad prided himself on living within his means, in having no debt, even paying for his cars in cash. That he felt he couldn't afford Smith by his own merits was uncomfortable for him, a humiliation. Smith was beyond him not only financially, but also intellectually and socially. He had an Associate's Degree from Wentworth Institute of Technology earned by going to night school—not a four-year Bachelor's degree from an Ivy League college. I would be socializing and bonding with people outside my family's socio-economic orbit. Smith threatened the balance in the familial mobile.

Mom chimed in with a solution to his objections and with a way to impress on my father his daughter's desire to go to Smith: "Jane, your spending money will be your responsibility. You will have to work summers for that, and you will have to sew your own clothes if you want things we can't afford."

Without hesitation, I assured my mother I was more than willing to assume that responsibility.

Dad's issues of clothes and spending money had been addressed and resolved. To boot, my willingness to work for spending money and sew my own clothes underscored for Dad my desire to go to this college.

Now Mom would deal with Dad's feelings of inadequacy that he didn't have the money in his wallet to pay the tuition. Ingeniously, she made the fact that he would have to work overtime a "feather in his cap" rather than the "black eye" he perceived it to be.

She said: "We can tell how much you want this, Jane, and it certainly is a great opportunity to go to such an illustrious college, but ultimately it's your father's decision for he will be the one who will have the real burden of your choice. It is he who will have to work overtime, going into the office on his Saturday mornings, to make the money to cover the additional cost of such a place as Smith. If he is willing to take on this burden, you will owe him all the gratitude for your attendance at Smith."

"Oh, I know, Mom."

Mom knew how to phrase things to achieve the goal. Dad hadn't liked this situation, but now he had power: power to grant or deny the wish of his beloved daughter. The fact that the money wasn't already there, that he would have to consent to work overtime to get it, only magnified his control of the situation rather than his impotence. He had the 'power to work overtime' to give something his daughter wanted!

Finally, Dad said: "Ok, Jane, if you really want this, it's ok with me."

"Really, Dad? Oh, thank you! THANK YOU!"

Since it was my father who was the deciding factor, I owed him one. I owed my mother too—but primarily for her intercession with Him.

My debt wasn't monetary, though money might have been welcome if not presented as a threat to Dad's pride as the primary provider. No, it felt like more than that. It felt as if I owed Dad life-long gratitude for the sacrifice—I owed for the gift, gratitude based on a recognition and acknowledgment that without Him there was nothing. Without Him, I would not have my newly acquired, elevated position as a Smith College student. Instinctively I perceived a filial covenant which could not be voided, or avoided, a contract which was tacit, understood and binding though unwritten and unsigned, a contract my mother had designed and described and to which I assented to attend Smith.

Implicitly, it involved a denial for all time of equality amongst and between us. And ironically, the money they gave me to obtain, through education, my escape from the limitations of my socio-economic background was conditioned upon a tacit pledge of eternal, filial indebtedness, "eternal daughter-ness." I had no sense that my parents had any innate, parental obligation to help me reach my potential. Instead, I perceived their financial assistance as a completely gratuitous act.

The impression I got from Smith alumnae at a prospective students' tea was that Smith would allow me to transcend the recessive, subordinate fate of most women. My parents had not met these confident alums, but they appreciated that Smith represented a different social, intellectual and financial world from theirs; that my exposure to this new world presented the possibility that I might be lost to them. Perhaps that is why Mom emphasized the sacrifice that was being made to send me to Smith, to introduce a tie that binds. Whether that was her reason or not—I didn't need that tie. I loved my parents—but I did feel the enormity of the debt.

*

Introducing me to Dave Barry, a Princetonian, Mom was probably thinking this was an appropriate, potential husband. He fit the bill. She hoped that by their making the sacrifices to send me to Smith, I would find a man like this: someone from one of the Ivy League men's schools, from a White Anglo-Saxon, Protestant family—with money and social standing: a doctor, or a Harvard professor, or perhaps a lawyer, in any case, a gentleman. We would move into one of the elegant, venerable, colonial homes in Concord, or perhaps Lincoln or Dover, Massachusetts,

24

towns that were just a *hop, skip and a jump* up the road from where I grew up—in fact on the route I always took for bicycle trips when I was a kid—but on a different planet from Arlington. My family would have made it, achieved the American dream.

I don't know when I first heard this ditty: *A son is a son till he takes a wife; a daughter's a daughter all of her life*, but I know I heard it from Mom and I got the message: as a daughter I would probably eventually become a wife and mother, but these identities would not, should not, conflict, prevail over or obliterate my interest, affections, identity and obligations as a daughter. My mother was telling me that I would always have the duty, and if I were a truly good girl, even the desire, to come home regularly, to keep the ties strong to my nuclear family—to in some sense, remain a child. Somehow, miraculously, this sort of permanent or eternal daughterhood wouldn't clash with my assumption of female adulthood. Female adulthood as I understood it seemed to contain room for this contradictory childlike state.

But, even if this David Barry from Princeton is the right guy, I thought, *I don't think I will be able to pull off this version of my future, because I'm not even good enough to graduate from Smith!*

Desperate to escape, I smiled: "Yes, it is a great place and I, too, am enjoying it, but you'll have to excuse me. I need to get home to work on a paper that's due tomorrow." I extended my hand to shake his: "Nice to meet you, David. Take care."

Having complied with her desire to introduce me to this "David Barry," I hoped my mother would say goodbye to him, too, and let us go home. She did, but on the way home she lobbied hard.

"Yes mom, he seems like a perfectly nice guy, but don't you think that he's way too old for me? I mean, he's MISTER Noble's college classmate! How old is MISTER Noble? He must be at least 25! Right?"

Mom had served on the Search Committee when the church hired Rip two years earlier: "He's either 25 or 26. That's not too old, Jane. Your

Dad is 6 years older than I am..." Then, with a coy smile emerging: "I think he likes you, Jane. I bet he calls and invites you out."

"Well, I think that he's too old for me! If you like him so much, Mom, YOU date him!"

"Don't rule him out without giving him a chance, Jane. You never know..."

Mom was right, as usual. That night he called and asked me out to the Boston Pops. I acceded to her encouragement to give him a try and though dubious of the outcome, accepted his invitation.

Mom would live to regret her advice.

CHAPTER 3

Dad and Mom were waiting for me in the living room as I descended the stairs. They were anxious to see the yellow coat on which I just put the finishing touches. David Barry would be arriving soon for our first date. He was taking me to the Boston Pops "Smith College Night" at Symphony Hall after a dinner at Locke-Ober's. My mother told me this was a very expensive, old world, Boston restaurant which, of course, neither I, nor she, had ever experienced. This was the life my Mom wanted for me and while I wasn't all that thrilled to see David Barry again, I agreed that the invitation was alluring and glamorous.

"Oh, I love it, Janie! It looks gorgeous on you...and so perfect for a spring evening," Mom, all smiles, burst out on my appearance.

"Yeah, I think it came out great too, Mom! Thanks for the fabric!"

I was proud of my creation out of the bright yellow wool that Mom had bought for half price at a Jordan Marsh fabric sale. I had paid much attention to my attire for this occasion: the yellow coat with the jewel neckline and white buttons down the front over a 'little black dress.' I made both of them.

I had been sewing my own wardrobe since age 12, shortly after I was introduced to the manual, non-electrified sewing machine called *a treadle*, which my mother inherited from her mother. Big, black, industrial, a monstrous looking contraption but ironically emblazoned in gold letters with the innocuous name, "Singer", it had sat silent neither growling nor singing in the cellar since my maternal grandmother's death a decade or so earlier.

One day when I was 10 or 11 my mother brought me down the cellar stairs to make its acquaintance:

"That's your grandmother's old sewing machine," she said, pointing timidly toward it as though if her finger got too close, the machine would rise out of its inertia to devour it.

"How come you don't use it, Mom? Can you make clothes with it?" I asked eagerly approaching it and running my hand over its strong, lustrous, black form. We never had much money, so the possibility that I could have more clothes without the obstacle of shopping, was tantalizing.

"Your Grandma used it to make clothes, but I haven't the slightest idea how to work that thing," my mother replied, the esteem with which she held her mother, my Grandma's talent, apparent. "I've tried many times to get this thing to work, but you've got to coordinate the pumping action just right to get it going. I'm not coordinated enough. I can't seem to do it. I get scared. I'm afraid that if I am able to start it, I won't be able to stop it and I'll sew my fingernail or something." She giggled nervously.

I felt her terror that she couldn't control it—that it wouldn't obey her will. But I didn't like recognizing it. To know that my mother was afraid of something like a sewing machine of all things made me uncomfortable and sad and angry. *I am her daughter. She is my mother. She should not be afraid of something...especially of a dumb machine. She should be strong, brave, smart. Why isn't she? What's wrong with her?*

"Oh Mom. Don't be silly. I bet *I* can get it going. Can I try?" I asked feeling very capable and proud of myself, but sad and disappointed in her at the same time.

Looking back, I think she showed me that machine with the implicit hope and maybe even the expectation that I, even at my tender age, would be able to accomplish what she in her mid-thirties felt she couldn't.

I was confident that I could get it going because my parents always told me that I was more like my dad than my mom. Yes, I would be 'feminine' but I would also be able to *do* things that men do, like athletics, driving a car, having a career.

28

Maybe it was because I was their first born, and perhaps their only child since my mother had had two miscarriages before I was born, that I should be everything, an extraordinary girl. After all I might be the only son they never had! In any case they led me to believe that I would not only fulfill all the expectations of a girl child—be sweet, obedient, graceful, popular, pretty—but I would also be as capable as any boy. So as if on cue, I proudly answered her expectations and got the contraption going. That led to sewing lessons and ultimately to my lemon-yellow coat for my first date with David Barry.

The requisite pearl necklace and earrings given to me by my parents at my high school graduation were my sole jewelry accessories. Short, white leather gloves and black patent leather pumps finished off the effect. In this outfit I was the image of the WASP stereotype we cultivated. Between Mom's periodic forays to Jordan's and Filene's Basements and my sewing skills, we produced very convincing costumes, succeeding so well that when Dave met my family at our church that fateful Sunday morning, he perceived us to be wealthy pillars of the church. He was quickly disabused of that impression when he arrived at our modest bungalow for our first date. He thought he was at the wrong address.

"I'm sure that you will make quite an impression on this David Barry," said Dad.

At that moment, the doorbell rang.

"Speak of the devil," said Dad smiling conspiratorially as he got up to answer the door.

Mom and Dad had just had a new, seafoam green, plush, broadloom, wall-to-wall carpet installed in our little living room. There had been some rain in the afternoon so Mom had made sure to put a remnant of it inside the front door so that anyone daring to enter our house with its pristine carpet could wipe his wet shoes so as not to sully it.

Before Dave could even say a word—or more importantly, take *a threatening step*—Mom greeted him pointing dictatorially at the remnant:

"Hi David. Please wipe your feet! WIPE YOUR FEET!"

Stopping short at the open door, his momentum almost causing him to fall headlong into the living room, startled, he looked up at us all, bewildered for a second. Then, he looked down at his guilty feet and it registered. "Oh!" and he dutifully wiped.

"Hi Dave. Come on in." I smiled sympathetically encouraging him to enter.

He was looking good, better than I remembered: tall, dark hair done in a classic Kennedy style—and not looking bald—at least not from the front—nice build and a really handsome, classic, dark suit, white oxford cloth shirt, striped tie and black wing tip shoes. He appeared the epitome of the poised "gentleman caller." I could tell Mom was duly impressed too.

He greeted us and almost immediately asserted politely, yet firmly: "Mr. and Mrs. McCall, we have 6 o'clock reservations at the restaurant, so we have to get going right away. I look forward to making your acquaintance more fully the next time we meet." Then, he turned to me: "Jane, are you ready?"

Right away I had an indication that the conservatively conventional suit was not the whole story when I tried to get into his car, a beat-up Chevy Corvair. The front passenger's seat looked like the contents of a trash barrel had been dumped on it. As I hesitated, he quickly scooped up the detritus and cast it into the back seat. I cautiously sat down in my nice, new, lemon-yellow coat, hoping that it would remain nice, new...and lemon-yellow.

I discovered that night that Dave's appearance was indeed deceiving. Underneath the conservative facade there was an eccentric. In his own words over dinner Dave told me he was born "with a silver spoon wedged firmly up my ass"—and he had chafed at the strict conventions that prevailed in his oh so proper world. It was a world in which there was little flexibility. Dinner was served by maids at precisely the same hour

30

every night. If he wasn't present, he didn't eat. He wore white on the tennis court, black on Sunday, only frequented the White Only theaters in Jim Crow Washington, D.C., attended specific, pre-ordained schools.

In reaction he confronted most rules. He was anything but the conventional type my mother and father assumed him to be. As we became acquainted on the drive into Boston, I grew increasingly interested in this iconoclast.

As Dave and I were led into the Locke-Ober dining room with its formal Victorian wine and gold wall covering, champagne white linen tablecloths, crystal chandeliers and sconces, rich, dark hardwood floors and abundance of luminous silver platters, Dave called my attention to the men's grille where I glimpsed what appeared to be a shiny, mahogany bar.

"It would be nice to go in there for a cocktail before dinner, but we can't. They don't allow women in there. Isn't that ridiculous?"

This guy is different from anyone I have ever known—from an upper crust family, the type of people we only see in Bette Davis movies, but also a genuine intellectual, steeped in Latin and Greek learned in a private boarding school. AND he's traveled the world AND he is psychologically deep and sensitive. I think I like him!

*

I made note of his comment about the men's grille and related it to a fact gleaned during our dinner conversation. He told me that his father had suffered from alcoholism and died when Dave was only eleven years old, depriving him of much of the usual father/son bonding. By default his mother had become the decision maker for the family. Despite his affection for his dad and his sadness at his loss, Dave hadn't seemed to assimilate the standard idea of the automatic supremacy of fathers, the idealization of the male. I found myself intrigued and attracted by his attitude.

31

Still, I was anything but a feminist. In fact when confronted by the likes of one of my Smith housemates, a chic, highly sophisticated, New York intellectual, imbued with feminist zeal, I was always uncomfortable, threatened by her activism. She constantly urged anyone willing to listen, to get involved in the struggle for equal rights. While I agreed with her premise that we women—especially Smith women—deserved equal treatment, did we need to be confrontational, to fight with men for it? Why couldn't we each, individually, work hard, compete and prove our worth?

Whenever the subject of sex discrimination arose at Smith, I assured myself and anyone else in earshot: "We don't need a confrontational mass 'movement' to achieve our goals of equality. If each one of us exceptional women simply works hard and stands up for herself, change will occur peacefully and naturally. We can have what we want." I believed that I was an exceptional female and that I and other exceptional females would achieve exceptionally.

In high school, hadn't I managed to thread the needle, to be non-confrontational, socially acceptable, yet compete academically with the guys as an equal? I was a traditional, pretty, pleasant, girl and still enjoyed equality of sorts with the boys at least intellectually. I didn't need to burn my bra like the rabid feminists my mother and I saw on the television news as I was growing up. Mom would exclaim: "Look at those crazy women! Why they are actually *burning their bras.* They're nuts! What's their problem?" To my mother, anyone burning perfectly serviceable undergarments they paid good money to buy *must* be nuts! Never mind ideology. The symbolism be damned. Mom rejected them as neurotic, unhappy troublemakers. This is the image of feminists I brought to Smith in the fall of 1964, that of unhappy, unhinged women-not justifiably unhappy because of the restrictions of sexism—but simply, naturally unhappy people.

My activist housemate's existence did contradict the image of feminists I garnered from my mother. *Here was a young woman, a beauty, who was popular with the men, seemingly happy, fulfilled, sane and intelligent, yet she espoused proactive, group confrontation against what she saw as a sexist system.*

While I didn't participate in her Women's Lib efforts to promote social change, I did embrace the idea of "liberation" from traditional roles, was energized by the ideal of equality and the possibility that I might actually live it. When I was around women like my Smith housemate who were vocal about sexism and the need to fight for women's rights, I felt somewhat sheepish. I sensed the inconsistency between my personal goals and desires and my reticence on the subject of women's rights in general. Inside a muffled, almost inaudible voice whispered the word "traitor."

Before I encountered my housemate's consciousness raising activism, there was the general tenor of Smith that I experienced immediately when I arrived on campus in the fall of '64, a year and a half before my Locke-Ober dinner date with Dave. I had brought with me, proudly and nostalgically, my somewhat tattered, homemade, red and gray crepe paper, cheerleading shakers. As I decorated my room that first day, I affixed them prominently to the mirror above my dresser, the place they had resided in my bedroom at home in Arlington. It wasn't long before some of my newly met housemates appeared in my room to chat. One approached the dresser pointing at the shakers. Smiling, she ribbed me: "Hey, Janie! You still going to be a cheerleader here at Smith?"

What had been unequivocally a badge of honor in my old world, my assurance that I would be socially acceptable even if I were an achiever like the boys, was not only not needed now, but at Smith it was like the scarlet letter or a red badge of shame. At Smith we young women had the right—nay, the obligation—to be one of the players or at the least to cheer for ourselves and for other women. That right or obligation may have been restricted to our campus, but there, at least, it was in effect.

At Smith, cheerleader shakers were not acceptable for liberated women but would liberation, power, equality be compatible with social, marital acceptability? The waters were becoming muddied, treacherous to navigate: too conventional and you didn't fit in this new world; too liberated and there may be societal consequences. Freedom, power, equality had its risks.

*

But this David Barry seemed like a prospective mate who welcomed an equal partner. That he so openly espoused equality was very attractive and exciting. With him there would be no need to fight for equal treatment.

CHAPTER 4

The Boston area, Arlington in particular, was the "best place in the world", and Newland Road (where my sister and I grew up) was where "truth" lived, too. Protestantism and particularly Congregational Protestantism was the "true religion"; men earned the living; women took care of the domestic duties; men mowed the lawns; women planted the flower gardens; men ran the church finance committees; women organized the church fairs to generate more money for the finance committee to manage. Things were black and white in my childhood world.

From Religion 101 my first semester at Smith, despite the fact that I understood little of the fine points of theology, I did realize that Park Avenue Congregational Church and the lessons learned there were, in fact, not the only truth; that there were many religious opinions only one of which my church espoused. At Smith, I was encouraged to determine my own definition of the truth. Smith College with the likes of feminists and Religion 101 blurred the picture, changing the blacks and whites of Arlington and my home to gray, qualifying everything, creating lots of doubts about the unequivocal accuracy of the world-view of my parents, leaving me with myself as my own, final authority, an exhilarating, but somewhat frightening and daunting situation.

After our Locke-Ober date, Dave became my steady boyfriend through the rest of college. Between his iconoclasm and my experiences at Smith, all the assumptions, all the doctrine learned in my childhood world, came under scrutiny.

In the spring of '66, my sophomore year in college, my mother and I were on the phone:

"Hi honey, it's Mom. I'm just calling to let you know that Dad has been in the hospital but he's just fine and home now."

Though her tone was matter-of-fact, black and white, with no hint of ambiguity or urgency, I was confused and shocked. *If everything is "fine," why is Mom calling me? This call is expensive. She would never invest the fifty cents in a long-distance phone call in the middle of the week if it weren't important, if something weren't wrong!*

And Dad sick? Dad is in his 40's, robust, the picture of health, strong.

"What's wrong with him, Mom? Why is he in the hospital? Is he okay?" The questions came tumbling out, one after the other, not allowing any response from her.

Seemingly exasperated by my intense probing, Mom answered each question without a break: "I *told* you: he's not *in* the hospital, Janie. He's home now. He's absolutely fine...it's just that he...fell off the ladder when he was putting stuff up into the attic and broke his collarbone."

I heard her hesitation. Our attic was only accessible by a pull-down ladder contraption in the hall outside my bedroom. The ceilings weren't very high, eight feet at most and Dad was six feet tall. It was hard to imagine how he could injure himself severely enough to be hospitalized.

"How did he do that, Mom? Did the ladder break or something?"

"No...." She paused. Again, the hesitation. For a moment she said nothing, then "Uh...no..., uh...your father had 'a spell' when he was on the ladder, but he's just fine now. Everything is fine!"

"But what do you mean a 'spell,' Mom?"

"Your Dad blacked out and he had something like a convulsion."

On several other occasions I had heard about one of these 'spells' occurring, but somehow, because the subject was dealt with cursorily, because I never saw Dad sick, because it had always happened when I wasn't present and probably because I didn't want to know he was sick, it didn't seem important. I never pursued what it meant. I simply heard what I wanted to hear...that there was no problem.

Helen, a housemate friend of mine at Smith, overheard my conversa-

36

tion with Mom. A no nonsense Midwesterner, she turned quizzically to me when I got off the phone, her eyebrows knit in bewilderment, and a slight grimace on her face: "Jane, *what* is a '*spell*'?"

I hesitated. Mom told me with such authority that this was a spell, but Helen was really smart, so her unfamiliarity with 'spells' suddenly made me wonder. With a gnawing sense that I was about to sound ridiculous, that I was going to sound as if I were talking about witchcraft or something, I responded didactically:

"Well, Helen, a 'spell,' is when you black out and have something like a convulsion. Dad's had these a few times before."

Helen listened patiently and then gently said: "Jane, you know that if a person has convulsions, he probably has epilepsy."

Helen's words were like a slap in my face, totally unexpected and painful. I was reeling. "WHAT?!!! EPILEPSY?! NO! NO, MY FATHER DOESN'T HAVE EPILEPSY, Helen! What are you talking about? He just has an occasional 'spell'..." *If Dad had epilepsy, I would know it. My parents would have told me.*

Of course, Dad *was* epileptic, but it took Helen—and then Dave— to conclude this from my description of events, before I would even entertain the possibility, before I would do the research to verify it.

When I went home during vacation, I discussed this with Mom face-to-face. Even when I pressed her, citing the information that I had researched, she adamantly denied that Dad was an epileptic:

"No, Jane, don't be silly. Your father is NOT an EPILEPTIC! He had Spinal Meningitis during the war. It left scar tissue on his brain which sometimes causes 'spells.'"

To preserve the idea that there was nothing wrong with Dad, that everything was fine, that Dad was well and strong and able to protect her and our family as the leader of the pack, Mom couldn't admit he was unwell. Beyond the social stigma, I realized that if it were known that Dad had epilepsy and took no medication for it, his driver's license

37

might be revoked, a family catastrophe when Mom was afraid to drive, or pretended to be, and virility was based on one's being the driver.

*

According to Mom, shortly after their marriage, she had had a minor fender-bender with a municipal bus, an event which according to her own report so traumatized her that she never drove routinely again. That one accident convinced her that she could not safely direct a car. An automobile, like the sewing machine, was beyond her control. Still, she annually renewed her license with great ceremony, but she rarely drove. And although she didn't choose to drive, she was proud to display her right to do so. It was as though she were saying: "I'm not driving now, but anytime that I choose to, I may. I have the right."

It had always been high family drama on the rare occasions when Mom did decide to get behind the wheel. Every once in a while, when it was completely unexpected, Mom would, with a strange mixture of mischief and terror, turn to my father and say: "Hey, Ron, I think I'd like to try to drive a little." Invariably, Dad would acquiesce: "Sure, I'll pull over in a minute, Hon." As if performing a sacred, but futile rite, Dad would get out of the car and walk around to the passenger side while Mom cautiously slid over to the steering wheel. Usually she would insist on a lightly traveled road like the road to the town dump, even then grimacing and groaning at the challenge of it. She would fidget, moving her hands gingerly around the wheel as though trying to find a comfortable position without touching it, adjusting the seat, the mirrors. When she got everything arranged just right, she'd put the car into gear and as it began to move, she in contrast became totally rigid, immobile, seemingly paralyzed. The more the car moved, the more rigid she became and the calmer and more confident Dad appeared. He comforted and directed her. "Now, Peg, just relax." he'd say with an easy, fatherly smile. "The car's not going to bite you."

After about 5 minutes of inching along the back roads, she'd say "I've had enough." *She'd had enough? We ALL had*! She'd pull over to the shoulder of the road and relinquish the controls to my father with a sigh of relief and resignation.

Although Kathryn and I openly laughed at her nervousness, I was always inwardly cheering her on, hoping against hope that this time she would succeed. When she didn't, I secretly felt sadness, disappointment and frustration. I wanted to be proud of her, but she seemed to have no confidence that she could impose her will on that dumb automobile. On the contrary, she seemed to think that the car would drive wildly and kill her or perhaps take her to places she didn't want to go. Somehow, she would be powerless to stop it. I was embarrassed for her, for her impotence. I laughed to cover my embarrassment and perhaps to distance myself from her.

If she had the power to control that car, it would no doubt have taken her, and me, lots of places. Instead, she had to depend on Dad and friends. He took her most of the places she ever went—to church, to stores, to friends and relatives or to Manomet. And it was good she was rarely far from home because when she was, she was uneasy. It was a lost cause. She couldn't venture out on her own and even if she could have, she'd be so anxious she couldn't enjoy herself.

Driving wasn't something Mom was supposed to do. If she chose to drive regularly, a second car would have been necessary, something Dad's salary couldn't afford. Either that or Dad would have had to take public transportation to work, not just an inconvenience, but a humiliation.

*

Although I had done the research and knew the truth about Dad's illness, Mom persisted in intentionally lying to me. A rift was growing between us because Mom refused to acknowledge the truth. If I didn't accept her deception, she was angry. When I was a little girl and began to doubt the existence of Santa Claus, insisting on the illusion was appropriate and loving. But, now for her to deny the truth when I knew it, felt like a rejection of my intellect, of my ability to perceive reality.

CHAPTER 5

It was the fall of '69. I was writing a paper in an upstairs den in our apartment on the campus of St. Paul's School, the Episcopal boarding school in Concord, NH, where Dave was both an alumnus and a "Master," the school's term for a teacher. Dave had now been my husband for more than a year and my ally as I negotiated my evolving relationship with my parents.

We were married in August of '68 after I graduated from Smith. Our courtship filled my last three years at Smith and his last two at Harvard Divinity School. It was an exciting time for both of us. Dave got to know my life and family and I his. My family was intact, no deaths in its nucleus; his was not, given his birth father's death and his mother's remarriage. His family was wealthy; mine was not. Every day was an adventure as we got to know each other and each other's background and family life. From the beginning we were both smitten. He told me I was beautiful and smart; I probably didn't tell him—girls didn't express their feelings as much in those days—but I thought he was socially sophisticated, good-looking and profound. And it didn't hurt that he was wealthy to boot.

From the time that Dave entered the door of my family's house only to be stopped short of the new carpeting, my parents were ambivalent about him. They were always positive about his financial prospects but they were suspicious of him as a person, baffled by what they considered his family's seeming lack of intimacy. When his parents visited him, they stayed at a hotel, rather than in his apartment; when he left home for the airport, his parents didn't drive him and linger at the airport window, waving, as he boarded the plane, they hired a livery service and said goodbye to him at the front door as he left for the limo. Mom's assessment, (really her indictment of him): "Dave's different."

When he visited Manomet the first time, Dad was mowing the lawn. At lunch, Mom suggested that 'Dave might help Ron out by finishing the job after lunch'. Dave had no idea whatsoever of how to use a power lawn mower and told my mother so. She was shocked and thought him spoiled. He thought she was rude to ask a guest to mow her lawn! If he had acquiesced and managed not to mow his foot off, he probably would have done the lawn the way he did it a few years later when we bought our first home.

Several hours after he went outside to mow, I looked out the window to see clumps of un-mowed grass scattered all around the yard. It looked as though it had been mowed by a goat. Dave had just wandered about with the lawnmower, not mowed in rows. The neighbor later told us he thought Dave was drunk. I realized that he had never mowed, nor cared to pay any attention to how it was done.

Needless to say, the different worlds we came from caused tension, not just between him and my parents, but sometimes also between him and me. Many times we had to learn from each other by talking out our different expectations.

This tension was evident to Mr. Canaday, the minister of my family's church. When Dave and I attended what was usually the 'pro forma' single counselling session provided by the minister as part of the fee paid for the marriage ceremony, the minister suggested "Let's get together again." This was unusual and not a function of his enjoyment of our company. Mr. Canaday was anything but a social butterfly. He was a serious, shy, intellectual, what in those days I would have called a 'nerd'. After the second session, Mr. Canaday, suggested a third meeting. My mother was totally bewildered by this situation, not to mention humiliated at the thought that this would "get around." Then, there was the unwelcome possibility of extra costs. Finally, Mr. Canaday acquiesced to our marriage on the condition that "If you find the tension becomes too much, you promise to seek professional help." "We do" and he married us, dubious of our future.

Now, suddenly, Dave appeared in the doorway of the den in our apartment at St. Paul's, out of breath from his sprint up two flights. He was 29, handsome in his classic khaki slacks and white button down, oxford cloth shirt with its sleeves rolled up revealing his tanned, muscular forearms. He seemed intense, excited:

"Jane, you got a minute? I was just thinking..."

Dave was, and is, always thinking. He's always had a very active mental life. I chuckled to myself: *What now?*

He was practically jumping out of his skin with excitement: "Jane, why don't *YOU* apply for the Ph.D. program at Wisconsin *with me*? You're just as smart as I am! Then we can go to graduate school together and maybe even team-teach in a college somewhere afterwards."

At the time, I was in a Master's degree program in English at the University of New Hampshire, planning to teach somewhere at the high school level. As I was nearing completion of that degree, Dave had started exploring the idea of studying for his doctorate in Byzantine history. I assumed that I would help support us by teaching on the secondary level. That he was proposing that we *both* get Ph.D.'s was a big deal. This was 1969. Few women were getting Ph.D.'s. Only recently had the idea of husband/wife university team-teaching been in the air. Although we hadn't discussed it directly much, this idea fit our tacit, revolutionary goal of sharing equally child rearing and money earning.

On my Smith graduation weekend, a year earlier when I found myself part of the traditional Ivy Chain the photos of which had so impressed me as an applicant to the college, I was convinced that I and my fellow classmates were a select group of women. Not only were we one of the first classes to graduate in the era of the modern women's movement, but given the benefit of our superb Smith education, I also felt we were

43

all elite, all exceptional women, destined to be those few women who were truly equal to the men, the few women who, I was confident, would soon join them as equals, as leaders in the workplace and in society. I envisioned equality between the sexes in the professional world and equal sharing of the household, child-rearing duties.

Immediately following my graduation and marriage to Dave, I, like many of my Smith classmates, energetically and idealistically pursued the goal of being a modern, "liberated" woman. One of the characteristics most endearing about Dave when we were dating was that, unlike most of my previous boyfriends, my hopes and aspirations weren't just words to him. He knew and embraced from the start of our relationship my desire and determination to be an equal partner.

Still, his suggestion that I, too, pursue a doctorate, dumbfounded me. Excited, thrilled, flattered, yes, but nervous, SCARED—all at once. I hadn't *ever* entertained this idea. In part that was because I had yet to finish my masters' thesis, but primarily it was because the idea was simply bolder than I was. Yes, I was interested in a career. Yes, I intended to break the mold of my mother's life, the housewife mold, but a Ph.D.? That seemed to me beyond my abilities.

I offered all the standard objections:

"Oh, we can't afford that, Dave."

"Me?! Get a Ph.D.?!"

"Huh? I'd never be accepted into the Ph.D. program."

I didn't think I was smart enough to earn a doctorate, a degree which seemed way beyond me. True, I had been an "A" student in high school, and had mostly "A's" in my master's work, but I didn't see an "A" my whole four years at Smith. Instead, I was a "C+/B-" student there, even spending time on "probation" at the end of my first year, beginning of the second. I didn't think my cumulative average would gain me entrance to a doctoral program. And if it did, I probably wouldn't be up to the task!

44

While I didn't say this to Dave, in reality, subconsciously I thought doctorates were for men, not women.

CHAPTER 6

It was ironic that I felt this way about the Ph.D. given that I had lived most of my life consciously considering myself different from most of my gender, living up to the image I perceived my parents had of me: that I would always be an exceptional woman.

Born in the era of strictly enforced feeding schedules, as an infant I had demanded and received—"against Dr. Moran's explicit orders"—as Mom so often reminded me with a rebellious twinkle in her eye, "on demand" feedings. In her reminiscences of my infancy my mother painted herself as an emaciated, wan, exhausted new mother, up night and day sterilizing baby bottles and preparing formula to satisfy the voracious, indelicate, distinctly unfeminine appetite of her infant daughter. As a child, prompted by her descriptions, I would visualize her engaged in a kind of slapstick, a Lucille Ball character, hair wrapped up in curlers, bottles and formula everywhere, in the midst of a home-style assembly-line gone amuck.

By the affectionate, amused tone she used to describe her long nights spent fulfilling my imperious dairy demands, I knew she approved of my insistent temperament as a sign that this child, even though female, would not docilely accept anyone else's dictates. This child would demand and obtain what she wanted in life. My mother seemed exhilarated by my forcefulness. If nothing else it prompted her to defy sacred, medical authority, male authority on child rearing. It was as though we had formed a successful, tacit conspiracy against the powers that were ordained to control us.

By the end of my first year the "on demand" feedings had produced a 30-pound baby. Since it was 1947 and I was short, rotund and ruddy faced, my parents thought I looked like a miniature Winston Churchill. When I was old enough to appreciate this association, it seemed loaded with significance. After all, they could more appropriately have compared me to rotund, Kate Smith of "God Bless America" fame, a female. Whether they intended it or not, I understood the comparison to Churchill as a statement that they thought of me as bright, a future leader—the equal of a great man.

For me, my superiority to my younger sister, Kathryn, was always implicit in my mother's constant comparison of me to my father, and Kathryn to her. I was "your father's daughter," "the apple of his eye." According to my mother he was unequivocally admirable. I not only had his coloring but she said I also had his relaxed, confident temperament and demeanor. Like him I was described as self-assured, intelligent, mechanically-inclined, logical, capable and excellent in math and science—"just like your father." Kathryn, in contrast, was compared to my mother and described as uncoordinated, not mechanically inclined, anxious, cautious, sensitive, emotional, somewhat diffident and more vulnerable.

Long before I was old enough even to apply for a driver's license, I knew I would be different from my mother. Both my parents told me so. Mom told me: "I know that when you grow up, Janie, you'll 'drive like a man.'" I heard the implicit "with confidence and self-assurance."

Someday I would easily direct machines anywhere I willed. Already I rode my English bike with its elegantly narrow tires at blinding speed as if I were a goddess of the wind. Long, brown hair fluttering like a cape around my shoulders, arms outstretched above my head in a show of effortless control, I reveled in the freedom, independence and power my bicycle afforded, responsive as it was to my every command. Swaying only the lower half of my body, no hands on the handlebars, I swept in a slalom motion down Bow Street and into the driveway of the big, brown two flat where we rented the second floor, for the return to my life as a mere mortal girl.

My dad had decreed my freedom. I had wanted a bike for several years, but Mom told me that I would have to wait until I was older: "Our street is just too busy for a youngster to ride a bike. You'll be hit by a car."

Was it her fear of the traffic or their tight budget that constrained her more? I didn't know. I'll never know, but one day Dad called me down to the driveway. As I approached him, he smiled conspiratorially and disappeared through the basement door, emerging seconds later with an elegant, shiny, dark forest green, English bike that emitted the requisite, rich tick-tick sound as he rolled it toward me. He was beaming with pride.

I had been wanting a Raleigh, spurning the fat, clunky frames of the American bikes. "Oh Dad," I squealed, "It's a Raleigh!" His smile faltered a bit:

"Uh...Almost....It's a Robin Hood...another English bike..." pausing for my reaction. "I LOVE it, Dad! It's beautiful!"

I didn't know it then, but Dad had bought the bike used. Evidently, he couldn't find a used Raleigh, but as Mom later told me, he spent every evening after a full day's work lovingly refurbishing every inch of that Robin Hood so that its perfectly burnished chrome gleamed bright as a diamond, and the green of the frame was as luxurious as velvet. Despite the fact that they had little money, Dad did everything he could to allow me to realize my dream of a bike of my own. I slipped onto the seat and sped away down the street lined with other two-family homes.

*

Mom was still fearful of my adventurous desires, worrying that I would get hit by a car. If it had been up to her, I wouldn't have gotten a bike. Her attitude reflected her own feelings of vulnerability and powerlessness. Judging by my mother, I had perceived that most women were impotent, thought they were impotent, or pretended to be impotent. Since I was always described as more like a man, more like my father, in personality and abilities, I didn't enter the mix. I was an "exception"—at least in my own mind. Women for me were—or behaved as if they were—not the equal of men, fearful, inferior and subordinate. They were not—or behaved as if they were not—as bright as men. They were—or behaved as if they were—less coordinated (less able to control or direct themselves and others), less mechanically-inclined (less able to control or direct machines and the non-domestic world in general).

There's a snapshot of my mother pregnant with me in the summer of 1946, perched like a child, herself, on my father's knee—the first of his "daughters". He was assuming a jaunty, self-assured pose on the front bumper of a snappy convertible as though it were his car, but ironically, it was the car of my mother's best girlfriend, Magnihild. Dad has a stylish pipe in his mouth, his elbow on one knee, his other knee serving as a platform for his impregnated wife. My mother's posture, in sharp contrast to his, is hunched, clingy; her smile ingratiatingly innocent. While he leans away from her, as if to display her, she leans toward him like a plant towards the sun, its source of warmth and strength. The relationship between them—the hierarchy which would ultimately lead to my estrangement from them both—was established already even before my birth.

If my perception of women came from my mother, my perception of men came from my father. But there was a hitch. There were two Ron McCalls. There was my perception of him and there was the image he assumed in the snapshot, the image my mother and he (but especially my mother) promoted to me, and to the world. That image was the man she wanted him to be: sophisticated, intelligent, powerful, superior.

For me my father was a gentle, loyal, handsome, physically strong, kind, not particularly articulate, unsophisticated kind of guy of above average intelligence and abilities. He spent much of his spare time in our basement smoking a smelly, soggy cigar (not the suave pipe of the snapshot), catching snippets—whenever the electric saw or hammer he wielded fell silent—of the Red Sox, losing yet another one. Every spring when the teams would begin strong, he would predict their ultimate demise, only to loyally, nay slavishly, listen to every game thereafter. His devotion to the Red Sox seemed appropriate. Like them he was lovable but sort of a loser when measured by the patriarchal standard. When he tried to assume the power role, he seemed to me inadequate.

My earliest memories of him involve the cellar at the two-family flat where my family rented the upstairs apartment in the '50's. Mom and Dad must have had some arrangement for a rent discount with Bea and Harry Bucknam, the elderly owners who lived downstairs, because I remember many mornings when I would accompany Dad as he went down to the old coal furnace, opened the creaking cast iron door in its belly and shoveled in coal from the dark and dusty bin nearby. It was spooky down there and the furnace was threatening, but with my father I had a sense that everything was okay. Dad was able to defend me from any evil being that might lurk in the gloom. When it came to the pipes, valves, gauges and the like that protruded everywhere in that cellar, Dad was brave. He had an air of competence about him. He understood these things.

I can barely picture my father in any situation that didn't involve some kind of manual labor. Often, he would arrive at the table for meals with sawdust on his head or dried specks of paint like confetti amidst the field of blonde hair on his arms.

Dad was a doer. He mowed the lawn; he painted woodwork; he built our cottage at Manomet to my mother's exacting, though cost compromised specifications; he drove us places; he packed and unpacked the car's trunk with methodical exactness for our trips to the cottage. On some Sundays he would cook breakfast or a Denver omelet for supper. His specialty was eggs.

It is this guy that I loved and miss to this day. This Ron McCall was the real McCoy, happy doing what came naturally to him—carpentry, auto mechanics, electrical or plumbing work. Here there were no pretenses.

Then there was the man in the natty tweed jackets smoking an aromatic pipe redolent of authority who looked as if he had just finished teaching a class in Shakespeare at Harvard—but when he spoke, "the jig was up." That man was my parents' concoction, their attempt to satisfy societal ideals, to make out of a rather unassuming soul, someone deserving to be the patriarch of a fancy family. In this 'persona' he left a desk, refinished impeccably by Ron, the handyman, in perfect order, full of financially important documents when he died. My mother had a desk, too, but hers contained photograph albums, our old report cards, yearbooks, baby books, her father's maroon Shriner's hat: the emotional stuff of life rather than the legal or financial. Not only were Dad's things sorted and stored neatly, but like-kind items were bound together with elastics and paper clips. This Dad knew where he wanted things and made sure they were there. Nothing would become disorderly if he could help it.

After his death—the ultimate in disorder—I searched his desk at my mother's request looking for his life insurance policies. Observing its strict order, I was reminded how in recent years he had always packed Christmas presents so securely for their journey by mail to Wisconsin that it would take a full fifteen minutes of frenzied frustration for us to get at them. He was a cautious, organized, deliberate, responsible patriarch.

Dad and I didn't talk much so there's not much memorable that he ever said to me. Mom was the primary communicator to us girls. Dad's one statement that reverberated through my childhood was "I love you, doll." He said that many times. And a couple of months before he died, he did say, through his tears of regret, that he was sorry for spanking me.

It was in his persona as family patriarch that this spanking would occur. In fact, in that role he hit me with his own belt, which hung on a rack on the closet door in my parents' bedroom. As a child, just the sight

52

of that rack struck grudging obedience into a willful, recalcitrant heart. My mother would point at it and threaten: "Just wait until your father comes home! You'll get the 'strap'." Occasionally she did the honors, but by and large, she deferred to Him. In later years when my parents spoke of "the spankings", they both declared that the ordeals hurt my father as much as they hurt me....I know they did hurt the real Ron McCall. And though the blows stung the flesh and my pride, he never did cause any cuts or bruises.

Ron McCall, the patriarch, was as much my mother's creation as my father's, a creation I always recognized as fraudulent. It wasn't that he rejected the idea of supremacy. It was simply that he couldn't fulfill the grandiose requirements of it and I knew that. When she would speak of him in hushed tones, inevitably in stock formulaic phrases, as "such a smart man," "so talented," (by implication more intelligent and talented than she), "the salt of the earth", "the best man that ever lived," a man who could "turn his hand to anything"—and "a wonderful driver," I would silently register one of two reactions. Either "God, I'm sick of hearing this. What a bunch of bologna." Or "What's the big deal that my father can 'turn his hand' to anything—whatever that means—or drive a car well?" Perhaps Freud could have provided the answer.

The things he did well were things many people did as well or better; the noteworthy characteristics attributed to him simply were fabrications or at the least exaggerations. Dad was an ordinary man, with good points and bad, yet my mother always inflated him into something more, something he wasn't. She touted him as superior simply because he was a man, because he was her husband, because he was Our Father, in essence a reflection in this world of God, I guess.

One of the activities he engaged in which best reflected these patriarchal pretensions was the Masons. I never understood the bureaucratic layers of that organization: how "the Lodge" he frequented when I was little was related to "the Masons," an organization which seemed to make its appearance in my teenage years, but the one thing I knew was that this was "men's stuff." Dad was very proud that several of his male friends served in an official capacity they modestly called "Grand Potentate." Their wives dutifully accompanied them to pretentious functions, balls and dinners, while the men ruled. When Dad would don his 'fez', a maroon hat fashioned of heavy felt and festooned with a gold tassel and a heavily ornate crest-like design, he looked comical to me, as if he were wearing an upside-down flower pot on his head—on his massive head. Whenever I would ridicule his appearance, he would inevitably become very serious and announce: "The Masons is not a secret society. It is a society of secrets." With that smug, cryptic pronouncement he would disappear out the front door for the evening with his fellow initiates.

It seemed important that "The Masons" was not a secret, that everyone knew it existed and that he belonged. It also seemed important that he had secrets and that we knew that fact. Somehow it was our ignorance of these secrets that made him and his "potentate" pals powerful, "potent". We were being told that this group existed; that it was important—in their own estimation and by their own account—and finally, that we couldn't get there from here.

When Dad died, his Masonic friends solemnly put a carpenter's apron on him for the wake. They appeared out of nowhere. In front of his casket and the gathered mourners like 'deus ex machina,' they performed a mysterious ceremony, apparently filled with religious significance connecting my father and his fellow Masons to Christ, the Holy Carpenter, to God, the Creator. This group evidently saw itself as a part of a divine continuum. Maybe that was the secret?

In my eyes the claim to power depreciated Dad. It made him ridiculous and pretentious. For me he was more noble when he was content with his humanity, with its vulnerability, with his limitations, simply doing what he liked, hammering, sawing, painting something for his family. It was then that he and I would watch "The Honeymooners" and roar together at the absurdity of Ralph Cramden and his "Royal Order of the Raccoons." Somehow Dad could see Ralph, Ed and the Raccoons as buffoons....

If in his incarnation as the patriarch of our household, my father was supposed to possess manly intelligence, virtue, strength and power; if he as the male was the final word, the leader of the pack, the head of our family, the only areas in which the women, my mother and sister, were supposed to excel were domestic and social.

My sister by age 8 was dubbed a good cook by our mother. I was told by Mom that I had no such talents. This was consonant with the fact that I was not a conventional female. I did sew, but that activity was portrayed more as a form of construction or manufacturing with an economic component rather than domestic, the female equivalent of building a house.

Personal relationships were female territory too. While my mother said that she and my sister had many friends who had great affection for them, I understood that I was popular, but that my relationships were more political than emotional. Although I was a female, somehow, I was a genetic aberration. On balance I felt that since I had received most of the positive male qualities, I had lucked out.

Much of my energy was expended proving my exceptional status and displaying that difference. On Sunday afternoons after church, my family and another family would often go on outings. Their son and I were in the same grade. During those excursions it became my obsession to match wits and athletic skills with "poor Eddie", a nice, quiet unassuming sort of kid, the unlikely son—a "junior" no less—of an aggressive, determined dynamo of a dad, the kind of man my Dad was supposed to be...but wasn't.

That his father was a hard driving, successful businessman in large measure accounted for my urge to compete with Eddie. By overcoming him, not only was I proving my own worth, that I was not just another wimpy girl, but I was also defending my family's honor. His dad was an employer of many men, the owner of a company; my dad was only an employee and a relatively lowly one at that. I was keenly aware of that. Mom was frustrated by it.

How many evenings do I remember my mother and father lamenting the promotion of other men over my father? My mother usually urged my naturally more passive father to be more aggressive. "Ron, if you don't toot your own horn, no one else will. You're more talented than _____ (Fill in the name. There were many over the years.), but he is always promoting himself while you are so quiet. You're too humble."

Eddie's dad was rich, or at least in my parents' eyes he was rich; my dad wasn't. His dad was a leader in local and state politics; my dad was not. In my mind as I challenged and conquered Eddie, I won standing for my family—something I always sensed my father hadn't done—though such an assessment would have been deemed blasphemy.

Most of the time I beat "poor Eddie" whether it was throwing, catching, running or computing. I even beat or fought him to a draw in hand-to-hand combat. I was a tough little cookie and I wanted him to know that.

To my delight he would often express amazement that I was actually a girl, telling me that he had told all the kids at his school about me. To salvage his own masculinity when I, a female, outdid him, he would have to depict me as a phenomenon. I cherished the idea that he considered me and portrayed me as different from the rest of the girls. That he perceived a difference was external confirmation of, and justification for, my identity as "an exception to the rule."

Still, I didn't want to sacrifice my feminine identity. My favorite outfit in those elementary school days was a red calico, quilted, circular skirt with glitzy rhinestones on the patch pockets. My mother's sister, glamorous, intellectual, Auntie May (pronounced "Aahntie May" in Arlington (Aahlington), Massachusetts)—another "exception" and the closest thing I had to an acceptable real life, female role model, had given it to me for my 8th birthday. I can see her now walking down Bow Street toward our second-floor apartment holding my Cousin Warrie's hand and carrying a bag containing my birthday presents. She had taken the Mass Ave bus up to Arlington Heights from her apartment in Cambridge, then walked the third of a mile to my street in her high heeled shoes. I would watch for her from the worn wing chair in front of our living room window, eagerly anticipating her arrival, transfixed by the spectacle she created. She was like a movie star, wrapped in furs—a mink stole or some sort of a fur boa. She would bedazzle. Her presence in my working-class neighborhood with its train track to Boston and the world beyond behind the two flats across the street was simply an event for me.

But what really made "Ahntie May" special was that she was not only good looking and glamorous—she was smart—and not shy about telling you that. According to her and my mother, May had been the smartest kid—boy or girl—at both the Agassiz School in Cambridge and Arlington High School. Reputedly, she had an IQ of 160. She had a presence about her—a huge haughtiness really—that differentiated her from my mother and most of the other women who populated my life. They were "good girls". Though I was certain that my aunt was a loyal mother and wife, completely monogamous, "Ahntie May" had a naughty air about her, a cockiness, (interesting that word "cocky), an irrepressible vitality, a liberation, that was lacking in the other women I knew.

Whenever I wore that red quilted skirt she had given me with a short-sleeved sweater which revealed the curve of my well-formed biceps, and tied a scarf tightly around my neck, cowgirl style, I felt cocky myself. Somehow that outfit, reminiscent of a gun totin', calf ropin' woman, embodied everything I wanted to be: physically beautiful—the consummate 'femme fatale'—but still spunky like a man. A woman to be reckoned with, an exception, a conventional girl, yes, but powerful and smart like a male.

Until the witching hour of puberty arrived, feeling "a woman to be reckoned with," exceptional, came naturally and there seemed no obstacles. I was an A student who sometimes joined in the touch football games the neighborhood boys played in the school yard across the street from my house. Since I was quick, had a ballet dancer's leaping abilities and keen eye-hand coordination, I was a talented tight end, almost always beating my male competition. I can still see myself streaking down the field looking up and back to track the ball. I knew I was different from the boys, but in my mind that difference only enhanced my celebrity.

One day in the summer of my 7th grade year, Mom observed: "My, your calves are really getting muscular, Janie. That must be all that toe dancing that you do. It seems to really develop your muscles. You should be careful...." Her words struck terror in my heart. She didn't directly proclaim the situation dire, but her tone and facial expression, the crease between her eyes, communicated the message. She didn't have to explain anything. Somehow, I had learned, simply by living, that muscularity in girls was unattractive. Big muscles were not pretty, not to be cultivated. Mysteriously, I seemed to have suddenly acquired the kind of muscles that develop quickly and easily with exercise. I had taken ballet and toe dancing lessons since I was 7 without a problem, but now all of a sudden at almost 12 my calves were becoming bulbous and as I noticed once directed to them, even, heaven forbid, faintly "veiny." I immediately curtailed physical activities like bike riding, toe dancing and running. I actually quit toe dancing altogether and every time I rode my beloved bike, I made a point of minimizing the number of strokes I took, coasting at every possible occasion. It was sort of a game I played: *how little can I use my big, powerful legs and still get to my destination?* I was becoming an adult woman and my legs refused to remain those of a young, petite girl.

I felt frustrated and bewildered by the necessity for my sacrifices, but perhaps that very genetic aberration which in my mind gave rise to all my positive male qualities had to be curtailed before it got out of hand

and made me too mannish? I was an exceptional girl, but I didn't want to be what I considered a freak—a muscular female. Given my "difference" it was extremely important for me to conform perfectly to the other specifications for femininity. Somehow, suddenly, my body wouldn't do that naturally.

For some time after my forced retirement from the field of play, I would wistfully peer through the chain link fence of the school yard across the street from my house at Larry Balboni, Richie D'Olympio, Bunky Doherty and Billy Smith, as they continued to play football and proudly display the power of their developing bodies. It was too dangerous for me to do that. Beyond growing muscles, reveling in my physical prowess risked either being considered a show off or threatening the guys' feelings about their virility.

So, I turned my energies to the one remaining venue where I could demonstrate that I was different from the other girls and competitive with the boys without being labeled strange in some way: the classroom. Even there, though, there were problems. It was tricky to combine exceptionalism of any kind with acceptance as a normal girl.

In response to the challenge that the Soviets posed with their launch of Sputnik, my school system was separating all us students into groups according to our intelligence. The brightest and/or most motivated kids were placed in a group called the AT class ("Academically Talented") slated to have learning accelerated. At a time when most of my girlfriends were beginning to focus their attention on bras, menstrual periods, boys and the lyrics to Elvis Presley's latest release, I set my sights on getting into the AT class.

Although I didn't want to be the typical, frothy female, I didn't want to be or look the book worm either. In my eyes most of the "academically talented" girls wore ill-fitting, unstylish clothes, ugly glasses and clumsy shoes. They seemed oblivious to, or purposely ignored, the conventional code of feminine acceptability. If not anti-social, they were generally unsocial. If prevailing wisdom deemed the physically attractive, sociable girls less intelligent and the intellectual, intelligent girls not dating material, I would continue to be the exception. I would be an academic achiever, but pretty and socially acceptable as well. In short, I would meet the conflicting demands of a basically conventional but ambitious family as it coped with the challenge of maximizing the possibilities of its fate—two female children.

While only my calves were developing, my best friend, Diane—who had competed with me for the title of best student each year of elementary school—was flowering into full womanhood. I remember the exact moment that I realized her metamorphosis; it was a pivotal moment for me. We were in the schoolyard playing softball during gym in Miss Russell's sixth grade class. I was on deck waiting my turn at bat. Diane was up. When she took a hard swing at the pitch, a thin strap slipped out onto her shoulder from under her sleeveless blouse. Suddenly, I computed: *That's a bra strap, not an undershirt strap! What's she doing wearing that?* I was eleven, young for my age physically, naïve psychologically...and hadn't consciously considered the possibility that my friends or I would soon grow up to become like our mothers! True I had heard a couple of girls talking about a "period" or something, but I hadn't really understood what was going on. I felt alienated, out of it. Mom and I hadn't yet had that discussion. I'm sure that given my still obviously pre-menstrual body, she felt such a discussion was premature, but in that moment of epiphany, I suddenly realized that Di was becoming like Mom. She was changing...and we were all going to change, too.

It was shortly thereafter, in the seventh grade, our first year in junior high, that my relationship with Diane as an intellectual rival ended. Mysteriously, her grades began to decline. She was struggling academically. We were both embarrassed to talk about it so we didn't. I was bewildered by the situation until the night of a sleepover at her house. Her family and I were gathered at the kitchen table having dinner. Diane's father, older than my Dad, with thinning gray hair and a ruddy complexion, seemed brusque and scary. Her little sister, about six years younger, was there too. Her mother was attractive, but not at all like my mother who had a natural look. Di's mother wore more make-up, foundation, mascara, lipstick, had honey, bleached-blonde hair, always perfectly styled, and fingernails that sported glossy polish and were amazingly shaped. She wore leopard prints, sunglasses with rhinestones, high heels and in general, though I remember her as an attentive mother, she reminded me more of a movie star than a regular mom. As she bustled about the kitchen, Di's father—who I knew was a Harvard grad, something very unusual in our working-class neighborhood—dominated all conversation. He seemed formidable to me as he asked me questions, speaking in a loud, stentorian voice and articulating each word with emphasis. I was thinking he must have taken elocution lessons, something that my mother said was very popular in the 1930's and '40's.

"So, Jane, how do you like Junior High West?"

"It's good. I like it."

"Are you taking the college prep course?"

"Oh, yes. Of course!"

"So…you are planning to go to college?"

I thought this was a strange question. In my house there was never any question that I would go to college. My parents were committed to that proposition. Because neither of them was a college graduate, their dream was that their children would be educated.

I answered him with what I was sure was the "right" answer, since he was a Harvard alum: "Oh, yes, of course, I'm going to go to college!" I smiled proudly, confidently.

Suddenly, his face changed from inquisitive to condemnatory. He became very stern: "Well, as you know, Diane is not going to go to college. I don't believe in spending my money to send a girl to college. It's a waste! Girls just get married and raise families—as they should."

I hadn't known....I was astounded. I looked to Diane for some reaction, but she was looking down at her plate moving her fork around in her peas and avoiding eye contact with anyone. I didn't know how to respond. It was clear that he was not going to change his mind and since I was raised to defer to adults anyway, I simply said: "Yeah."

That ended the subject.

I couldn't remember what we talked about after that. I was shell-shocked and afraid to express my opinion about anything given that I obviously was not able to judge what was acceptable.

Over the succeeding years I witnessed Diane's goals shift dramatically from professional to domestic, probably a function of her struggle with the relevance of her studies to a non-academic future and with the pain of her father's attitude toward her. His views bewildered and angered me. Just because she was a girl, he, a Harvard graduate, refused to spend his money to educate her? That was a shocking realization.

Di never did go to college. She married her high school sweetheart a year after we graduated. He was going into his senior year of college. Within two years she was a mother.

As a direct consequence of my parents' expectations, and in direct contrast to Diane's path, I not only pursued college but also chose all college prep courses, many of which had been traditionally, and still were, dominated by the boys, like advanced math, chemistry and physics. In the early 1960's I was one of a female minority in those classes at Arlington High.

As I strove to excel academically, I wanted to continue to be a conventional, socially acceptable female so I auditioned and became a cheerleader. Immediately, I was uncomfortable with the high-pitched, babyish sound of our collective voices. I sensed that if we sounded more like the males, we would be more powerful, more effective. I didn't share this particular thought with the other girls, but when I became co-captain, I argued that everyone on our squad should lower her voice an octave or so when cheering our cheers would better penetrate the crowd. Needless to say, the rest of the girls on the cheering squad were somewhat dubious about sounding like the guys but they acquiesced. While we cheered the males on as our heroes—our appropriate representatives on the field of athletic combat, ("Jimmy Driscoll, he's our MAN, if he can't do it, the team can. The team, the team, they're our MEN, if they can't do it, NO-BODY can!")—I wanted us to do so with the authority and effectiveness of men's voices. So, there we were on frigid days as well as balmy, dressed to conform to convention in skirts so small they would fit our 5-year-old siblings, trying to sound like a bunch of linebackers.

CHAPTER 7

Now, at twenty-three when my husband invited and encouraged me to join him in graduate school to go for my own Ph.D., insecurity reared its ugly head. As in my early days at Smith, I didn't feel worthy of exception status. Although Dave's college academic record was very similar to mine, he had no reservations at all about his qualifications. He felt entitled to be admitted to grad school. And he felt the same way about me. At his suggestion—at his prodding, really—I hesitantly applied for the doctoral program at Wisconsin.

When I told my mother, she asked:

"What are you going to do that for, Janie? You already have a Master's so you can teach through twelfth grade. That's plenty. Only women who are 'weirdos' get their doctorates."

Dad said nothing about my Ph.D. plans. In his silence, though, he said volumes. It's true he wasn't a loquacious type. My mother was the more verbal of the two; however, he wasn't a mute either. When he wanted to say something, he did. If he disagreed with my mother's verdict, I would know it. Actually, if he disagreed with her pronouncements about something of this magnitude, she might very well not have made them in the first place.

Now, it seemed, my parents wanted to consider me normal. But I still wanted to be the exceptional girl I thought they expected me to be. Somewhere along the line an identity I cherished and nurtured, my identity as "an exception," had become vulnerable. I could be an exception *to a point*—a point determined by someone other than me. My desire to get a doctorate seemed to go beyond that point with both my parents. Ultimately, they supported my matriculation at Smith, but this time there

65

was clearly no benefit in their eyes. Instead, they perceived my doctoral ambitions as making me eccentric; if anything, compromising my social position, even within the family.

When I was a high school student living at home, the son of a contractor friend of my parents was studying for his Ph.D. All I ever heard was how wonderful that was; how admirable Harold was; how brilliant. So naturally I struggled with their negative attitude toward my ambitions. I was hurt and irritated that they weren't encouraging *me*, considering *me* an exception to the female rules, a worthy doctoral candidate. *Was I exceptional or not? I was having real trouble finding me.*

At some level, my own inner voice, a voice which had little respect for women and now little confidence in myself, a woman, was an externalized echo of my mother's attitude. While I was trying to assume a liberated identity, charting a course toward the non-traditional career of college professor, rationally and consciously mouthing the progressive script that women should be treated as equals with men, I was experiencing profound doubt and insecurity. *Am I smart enough to do this? Do I have the right as a woman—is it even right, for me to be defying tradition, perhaps even natural law?* I felt conflicted: at some moments unsure of myself and my abilities; at other moments angry, bitter, feeling betrayed by my parents who were doubting my inherent worth and talent.

For my doctoral application I needed recommendations. Immediately, I identified my Milton seminar professor in my Master's degree program. He had pronounced me one of his more promising students and my paper for his course had become the seed for my Master's thesis. Optimistic that he would support my lofty, unconventional ambition I made an appointment intending to ask him to write for me. On the day of the scheduled appointment as I approached his office, one of the more commodious in the department denoting his seniority and relative importance, the door was open and I could see him at his desk.

As soon as he glimpsed me, he greeted me heartily:

"Now, Jane, what brings you here today?"

Every cell in my body was energized. I was confident, but also somewhat apprehensive, cognizant of the unusual nature of my request. Still, I was smiling:

"Well, Sir, I am here today to tell you that my work with you has prompted me to apply for the Ph.D. program at the University of Wisconsin-Madison. How do you like that? And I'd like you to write on my behalf. Will you?" I beamed, anticipating his pleasure at the news that one of his students had been inspired by him to continue in the field.

To my consternation, he seemed totally disconcerted. In fact, he actually gasped. "Oh my! Jane, I am surprised...I mean uh..." He sputtered. His brow knit, his mouth contorted as he chewed his bottom lip, obviously not pleased, but rather, perplexed, by my request. "Are you really sure this is what you want to do, Jane?" he asked in a benevolent but discouraging and skeptical tone. "I mean, you're such a nice, attractive, young woman—married and all. Do you really want to spend the time, money and energy getting a doctorate? Don't you want to be able to have a family?"

Is he seriously querying whether I have carefully thought through my decision? He seems to be making a genuine effort to dissuade me from pursuing this degree. He feels since I am married and attractive that I shouldn't do a doctorate; that if I do, I might not be able to be a mother!

I had worried that I might not be smart enough to be successful in a doctoral program. And he had just confirmed the validity of my concern because I obviously had totally missed the point, some very important and obvious factors that made my decision untenable: my appearance, my marital status...and my gender! Even my mother with only a high school education didn't miss that point! *How could I have been so dumb?* I was so shocked by his reaction that I could hardly speak. Somehow during the past year, I had understood that he considered me a promising scholar and was excited by my work. Now I was left devastated and humiliated. Intellectually, I recognized that it was nothing personal, simply a traditional attitude toward women doing a doctorate, but he was applying that attitude to *me*, the exception!

I didn't know what to do. So, out of habit, I did what I was raised to do. I was courteous and non-confrontational with my male elder. I hid my intense disappointment, my pain, my humiliation, my anger, my shock. But still, I persisted with my request. Cajoling, with an endearing tone accompanied by an endearing smile, both calculated to be ingratiating, I played the "cutesy" girl, the cheerleader, rather than an adult woman. Smiling and sweet talking, I assured him: "Oh, Sir, you know me, I can do both!"

After the initial sting and the astonishment at my professor's attitude, I dismissed him as benighted and old-fashioned, the product of an earlier era, an anachronistic anomaly, nothing to worry about or dwell on. I thought to myself: *He's a dying breed, so why waste time and energy confronting him? Plus, given my dependent position I certainly don't want to antagonize him. He is my ticket to the Ph.D.*

CHAPTER 8

The fall of 1970 found Dave and me in Madison, Wisconsin as first semester doctoral students. Suffering the stress that comes with studying for Ph.D.'s, we had followed the advice of the minister who married us. We were sitting in a psychiatrist's office for marital counseling to help us navigate the challenges of two of us doing our doctorates simultaneously. Adding to our stress, my parents were about to arrive in Madison for a two-week stay. Ever since they announced their visit, there had been heightened tension between Dave and me. There was room for them in our three-bedroom house. That was not a problem, but Dave objected to the length of their stay. Though I understood his feeling that two weeks was a long time, their drive to reach Madison from Boston was also long. Once there, understandably they'd want to stay a while. I was vociferous in defending their plan.

Dr. Gilbert, a portly man in his 40's with a bushy brown beard and a huge, gleaming baldpate, asked in a soft, caring, soothing voice how things were going with us. I described the situation and the tension. He listened intently and then gently inquired: "So, Jane, how do you feel about the length of your parents' proposed stay?"

"Well, they want to stay for a while because they are driving a long way to get here. Dave doesn't understand that, or if he does, he has no sympathy with the fact that they will be tired and won't want to turn right around and head home. Plus, they don't see us often now."

Dr. Gilbert said: "I understand what you are saying but how do you feel about the length of their stay?"

"My parents will be hurt if we tell them that they can only stay for a week. Don't you see? That's what Dave wants me to tell them. He says that if they want to stay two weeks, they should stay in a hotel the second week, but they can't afford that!"

Don repeated his question this time with distinct emphasis on the word 'you': "But, Jane, how do YOU feel about the length of their stay?"

I sat silent, frustrated, and now somewhat threatened by the question. I didn't know how to answer him. *Haven't I told him how I feel...?*

"But I...I've been telling you how I feel! Haven't I?"

In his gentle, but at this moment, insistent voice: "No, Jane. You've told me how *Dave* feels and how *your parents* feel. I am asking you how *you* feel?"

Now I understood him and I was alarmed because I couldn't do any better than I was doing. I was struggling internally to figure out how to answer his question, but there wasn't any me to answer it.... Suddenly I felt tightness in my throat and tears burning in my eyes. I was paralyzed. I couldn't speak. *I don't know how to answer him any differently from how I already have answered him.* I was confused by the question. I thought I was telling him how I felt but I was telling him how other people feel. I answered him the only way I knew how to at that stage: "I guess I don't know how I feel." *No. I don't know how I feel. I don't know how to know how I feel.*

I was panicked. There was no me separate from others. I was afraid even to attempt to find a distinct me. *Does one exist? Should one exist?*

*

The next time Mom and Dad came to visit was two years later, Thanksgiving, 1972. Dave and I had been living in Madison for over two years. We'd had a chance to settle into our own life and routine there. I had the dining room table all set for the Thanksgiving meal with the elegant Royal Doulton gold trimmed china and sterling silver flatware that Mom and Dad had given us as wedding presents four years earlier. I thought the room looked elegant. We had painted the walls a soft cream with a

70

blush of rose and put up some artwork that we acquired at the Madison Art Fair on the Square the previous summer, two still life paintings of fruit. Now under my grandmother's shiny, dark mahogany table we had an old, maroon and navy, Afghan Bokhara rug that I had unearthed in an antique store. Somewhat ragged, with an actual tear on one end and suitably worn throughout, the tribal rug still retained some of its original rich glory and the strong, dark, formal, geometric pattern was pleasing against the light oak floors of the room. I liked the look, proud of my décor, and the home I'd built with Dave.

Mom and Dad arrived just as I was putting the finishing touches on the table setting.

"Janie, how pretty your dining room looks. And you're using grandma's table!" In fact, it was the table that my mother had inherited when her mother died shortly after my birth. It was old, but in mint condition. As her gaze swept the room approvingly, suddenly, it stopped at the carpet. "What happened to your rug? It's torn!"

I could understand that Mom didn't appreciate the aesthetic. I was okay with that. She liked the plain, machine made, clean broadloom type of carpet. My tastes had gone in a different direction. I liked oriental rugs even when they were old and used:

"Oh, yes, I know Mom, but I got it really cheap and I love the look. I think it has a certain patina and old-world charm."

She looked skeptical: "Well, if you like old, torn things I guess it's charming! But I don't like that. I mean, Jane, it's old and probably dirty! You can't really tell with this kind of rug where it's been...."

I decided to let the subject go.

We moved on from the rug and had a nice Thanksgiving dinner, the first I ever cooked. Even though I mistakenly roasted the stuffed bird upside down, it seemed I had stumbled onto the secret of a moist turkey, because, truth be told, despite the fact that I had bought a generic brand, not Mom's beloved Butterball with its injected butter to insure moistness, everyone agreed that the turkey was succulent.

I was feeling ebullient about the success of the holiday meal when the next morning I was startled to discover that the Afghan Bokhara rug had disappeared from the dining room! Mom was sitting at the table sipping her coffee, preoccupied reading our local newspaper when I entered. I was shocked and bewildered by the missing rug. It was not something that one could overlook. It was the elephant absent from the room: "Mom, where's the rug?!"

"Oh, Jane, Dad and I saw that the trash was out today for pickup and we decided to dispose of it."

I couldn't believe what she had said. *Did I hear right? Did she just say that she and Dad threw my rug away? Who does that?* And then I was pissed. I could barely speak: "You did? Why...why did you do that?"

"Jane, it *really* was too old and deteriorated. I mean it was ripped and worn and you don't know who owned it before and what dirt might be in it. We thought it best to get rid of it."

I was so incredulous, hurt and angry, but I just nodded: "Oh."

Reeling, I went into the kitchen for coffee. I felt the familiar unwelcome tightness in my throat and hot, stinging tears coming up into my eyes. I was angry at the loss of my antique find, but really more pained by the lack of my parents' respect for me. I could accept that we would sometimes disagree on things: politics, lifestyle choices, aesthetics, but what was so discouraging was that there seemed to be no acceptance or even tolerance for me, for my opinions and choices. The rug was symbolic of the disconnect developing between us as I began to desire and exercise autonomy.

*

Three years had passed since my rug disappeared. Dave and I were still out in Wisconsin, working on our doctoral degrees, making our own decisions. I was sitting in my thesis advisor's office, in my customary chair amidst the familiar clutter of stacked library books and mugs of unfinished coffee. The warmth of the sun's glow filtered through the winter's frozen film on the large picture window. Noah was only eight years my senior, but balding, he looked much older. He was ready to publish a new edition of a poem which figured prominently in the dissertation I was writing.

I had developed a new interpretation of the meaning of that poem, a psychological interpretation of a scene which had always been taken literally.

As I was sipping my coffee, Noah began to talk while somewhat distractedly perusing some papers on his desk. Without looking up, he said: "Jane, you will be flattered to know that I have decided that my new edition will include your groundbreaking interpretation." As I digested this information, he approached my chair and handed me the sheaf of papers he'd been collecting.

"See, Jane, here are the citations of your thesis I have put in my new edition."

Seeing my name in print, the title of my thesis in print, was a thrill. His book was about to be published and he'd footnoted my thesis. He had named me and credited me. I appreciated that but until that moment, my thoughts had only appeared in my thesis manuscript. Now they were in Noah's book manuscript.

"Wow! This is something! But, how can you footnote my thesis when it isn't yet finished or published?"

"Oh, Jane, your thesis will be finished by the publication of my edition."

It occurred to me that my work would help make his edition significantly different from previous versions. It would distinguish his edition from all preceding editions. I guessed that was good, but I was feeling used, as though he'd had an ulterior motive as my advisor. As I absorbed this idea, I was beginning to feel defensive. The inclusion of my thesis in his book seemed to be a 'fait accompli.' I didn't explicitly express my discomfort. I just began mindlessly rummaging around for my belongings, picking up my books and my purse and mumbling: "Noah, I'm glad to see my work is contributing to scholarship in a meaningful way. That's great!" Rising from my seat, "Well, I've got to get going to a class. See you."

I hurried out of his office and down the hall, dazed, unsure of where I was or where I was going. I just knew I had to get out of the building. Somehow, I found my car and made my way home. I arrived distressed. Dave was sitting in the family room reading. I couldn't even engage in greetings:

"Dave, you'll never guess what just happened!"

I didn't want him to guess. I just needed to unburden myself right then.

"What? Not a car accident?"

"No, no, no! No car accident...No, Dave." The words couldn't escape fast enough. "Noah just informed me that he is incorporating my interpretation into his edition of the poem! He showed me pages with my name and the title of my thesis on them."

Dave listened intently and quietly while I reported. Then, he asked: "So? Is there a problem with that? Aren't you flattered?"

"Conflicted: I mean I *am* flattered that he felt it important to include my idea, but I felt violated, as though he were taking my idea without my permission.

"What did you say when he told you?"

I felt my cheeks getting flushed from embarrassment. Implicit in Dave's question was the notion that if I felt that way about Noah's announcement, it necessitated a response by me. I knew it did, but I also knew that I had been mute about my feelings.

"I didn't say anything. I didn't know what to say. I mean...I was so taken aback. It was so unexpected. I was flattered, of course, to think that he has such faith in my interpretation that he wanted to include it in his work, but I wanted to say 'NO, YOU SHOULDN'T HAVE DONE THAT WITHOUT OUT ASKING MY PERMISSION FIRST'…but…I didn't."

"How come?"

"I don't know. I guess that I was afraid that I don't have the right and that it would be selfish and arrogant of me."

Typical of Dave, he probed: "Why do you think you don't have the right? It's *your* interpretation of the poem. No one else has ever seen it the way you have. Why do you think it would be selfish of you to express your feelings about its dissemination?"

Even though I wanted to talk about the situation, I began to get flustered and angry with him. I was simultaneously distressed by what felt to me like Noah's presumption, but annoyed by Dave's insistence that I plumb the reasons for my own passive behavior:

"I don't know. I mean, I don't know the protocol in these matters! He probably has the right to use my idea in his book as long as he footnotes me. It's just that he didn't consult me first to see how I felt. He *announced* that he intends to use it. That doesn't feel right. But maybe I am being arrogant or too sensitive not simply to be grateful that my professor will mention me in his new publication. He did make the point that this is an honor. Still I don't think I really want him to use my revolutionary interpretation that I confided to him in his capacity as my thesis advisor. I mean, the idea is not yet in the public domain…and may never be. He wouldn't even know about it if he weren't in his privileged position as my confidant. He may have the right to do this without even telling me, but when he told me that he was going to include my interpretation without first having asked me and discussing it with me, I felt disrespected."

"So, are you going to go tell him this—that you feel that he should have consulted you first, not simply told you that he was going to include your idea in his edition?

Dave was forcing me to recognize that my hesitation to confront

Noah was not because I didn't have the right to control the dissemination of my own ideas while they were still private, not because Noah didn't have the right to include my interpretation in his edition once it was in the public domain—but rather because I felt and was acting like a child, unworthy of the right even to express my feelings or question my professor about his intentions. I needed to behave as an equal human being who expects mutual respect. Just because he was a male and my professor, and I was the student and a woman, didn't mean we weren't both adults and that this situation didn't demand an equal adult response from me. He had a right to present his intention to me. I had a right to assert that hearing—before my dissertation was even completed—that my idea was going to be used in his book was, rightly or wrongly, uncomfortable for me.

Humiliated by my own recognized passivity, I drummed up courage, and returned to his office. Waiting outside his door alone in the long, stark white corridor, I shivered with anticipation and nervousness. In the harsh lighting I felt as if I were a criminal about to be interrogated. I anticipated and feared that he wasn't going to like my questioning his intention to use my idea.

When his door opened, I made my way to my customary chair located cozily just a few feet from him. But this time was different. This time there would be no casual exchanges between us. I started, hoping that my pounding heart was not audible:

"Noah, this morning when you showed me the pages in your edition with my name and idea in print, I was very flattered."

Before I could continue, he interrupted: "Well, of course you *should* be flattered. Your idea is ground-breaking, Jane, and I won't send my edition of the poem to the publisher without referencing your new interpretation of its meaning."

I was feeling the pressure that that statement carried. *Should I tell him why I have returned to his office...to prohibit his use of the idea...at least for the time being? He's going to be irritated by my attitude...but I must. It's my idea. I want to determine when and where it is expressed.*

"Yes, Noah, I understand, but I was also uncomfortable at the revelation. Frankly, I was shocked that before my idea is even in the public domain, you've included it in your edition."

Our eyes locked.

I proceeded, scared by the challenge I felt implicit in his eyes, not feeling my entitlement but knowing that I had to express my thoughts and feelings, that it was important for my own dignity: "I have lived with the idea for a few hours and I've decided that I don't want it published right now. That would preclude my opportunity to introduce it myself. If you use it in your edition, any article or book I might submit after that would be anti-climactic."

"Uh...I don't understand...," he gasped. "*Jane*, this will allow you to get your name into print as a graduate student." He was genuinely bewildered that I would take issue with his plan. Then, suddenly, anger. He went on the offensive: "You should, in fact, be thrilled. You probably will never publish an article. Anyway, it's not as though you worked a lifetime for this idea. It came to you like 'a flash in a pan'."

I heard him justifying his decision to take control of—if not total credit for—my idea on the basis that I had the type of thoughts that come quickly, unpredictably; that in his estimation I really hadn't worked hard enough for this idea.

"Yes, Noah, it's true that the idea came in a flash of insight, but you know how much and how long I have been studying and struggling with that poem, uncomfortable with the previous interpretations. Yes, the moment of epiphany, of understanding, came in an instant of insight, but that moment was the result of lots of work and effort on my part."

I felt hurt that he was not giving me credit for my hard work, suggesting that I hadn't engaged in rigorous scholarship; I had and it was that work that produced my conclusion.

"In any case, I don't like your intention to present my idea in your edition before I even have the opportunity to place it in the public domain myself."

He assured me that his publication referencing my idea would not appear before my thesis was submitted to the public domain.

It felt good. I had succeeded in plumbing my own feelings about the situation, expressing them and acting on them, but it wasn't easy. I continued to struggle: *Have I done wrong, perhaps been petty to honor the feeling that I was being disrespected by his expression of his intention, before my dissertation was completed, to use my idea in his edition?* I may have been wrong. I may have been petty, but it was important for me to accept and validate my own feelings if only because it was uncomfortable for me to prioritize my feelings, myself.

CHAPTER 9

In large measure because of Dave's faith in my abilities, seven years out of Smith, I had my doctorate. Our dissertations with their black bindings sit side by side, "David S. Barry", then "Jane M. Barry" in Memorial Library at the University of Wisconsin-Madison. His thesis has been ordered many times online by others wanting to benefit from his work. I was solicited by the editorial board of one of the most prestigious journals in the world, to distill my dissertation into article form for one of its editions. It seemed I was certainly going to escape the domestic pigeonhole occupied by my mother and her generation. The goal of a modern, liberated life, which includes the traditional blessings of husband and children yet doesn't necessitate sacrifice of one's personal career aspirations and public 'persona,' seemed within my reach. I felt heady to be in the vanguard of "liberated women."

Unfortunately, however, Dave's and my dream of a joint teaching appointment at some college had become unrealistic. The Arab oil embargo rendered the academic job market nearly non-existent in the mid to late 70's, particularly in the arts. In fact, most of our Ph.D. colleagues in History and English were driving taxicabs or had taken other non-academic jobs for lack of suitable, university positions.

I did secure a tenure track position teaching "Business English" at a satellite campus in the University of Wisconsin system but the pay was paltry, $5000 per semester, and the commute long and treacherous in the severe winter weather especially since all the classes I taught were at night. I was risking my life when the job wasn't even really in my field.

One night in subzero temperatures with a fierce wind chill, my car suffered a gas line freeze on the dark county road home and came to a complete stop. But for the aid of another lonely traveler, a Good Samaritan, on the road late in the evening, I could have frozen to death. This incident prompted me to re-evaluate my situation. Working a dangerous job for peanuts with almost no chance of its leading to a meaningful appointment seemed to make little sense. The academic job market was anemic; there were so many Ph.D.'s looking for employment and almost no openings in the arts, I decided to make a dramatic career shift to real estate.

Shortly after I made this decision, I discovered that one of the men who was in the English Ph.D. program with me at Wisconsin had applied for the job from which I had recently resigned. When he asked me why I resigned, I told him that $5000/semester was too low; that I needed more money. Suddenly, his mouth dropped open. I assumed that he was surprised by my decision to leave 'academia' for business after achieving the Ph.D., but no, he explained that he was aghast because he had been offered a substantially higher salary for that same job.

I had my Ph.D.; he did not. I had college teaching experience—several years as a teaching assistant at the University of Wisconsin-Madison; he had none. I had a better academic background and was a better student. He knew all of this, contributing to his astonishment at the wage disparity.

I, too, was shocked and personally insulted by the blatant discrimination but I had already decided to move on to real estate, where I assumed I would earn as much as I deserved. So, I decided not to make an issue.

Dave, too, at this time was experiencing the consequences of the glut of Ph.D.'s and the paucity of positions available. As a Byzantinist, his specialty was eastern medieval history. If there were any jobs available at all in medieval history, they were in western medieval history and there were loads of doctoral candidates in that area better qualified than he, an eastern medievalist, to take those openings. As Dave considered his options in this disastrous academic market, his Bachelor of Divinity from Harvard earned during our courtship seemed to hold the best career opportunity for him. Since his stepfather was a clergyman, Dave was familiar with this path though hardly a natural for the role. He didn't seem to have a vocation to be a priest. In fact, he was more agnostic than Christian. Further, he didn't like dealing with the sick or dying, a standard pastoral duty; nor did he like dealing with the poor. But otherwise, he was a perfect fit.

In pursuit of this course, Dave was exploring the Episcopal priesthood. I found myself sitting with him in the office of a certain Father Bach at a local Episcopal church. The thought of being a cleric's wife still didn't thrill me any more than it had when I first met Dave at Park Avenue Congregational Church in Arlington, MA and my mother introduced him as a Harvard Divinity School student. Not only did the role seem terribly restrictive, requiring me to be solicitous of the well-being of his whole congregation, but more significantly, I had hardly been in a church since I escaped the mandatory Sunday services of my childhood. If anything, I had become aware of the distasteful, patriarchal character of the church. At that time I knew of no female ministers or priests and of course the Bible portrayed the loss of Paradise as the fault of a woman. I believed in a higher power but I wasn't sure I was a Christian or that I believed in the church. Still, I loved Dave, so there I was. Since he had a need not only to be gainfully, but also meaningfully employed, I wanted to cooperate.

We weren't in Father Bach's office more than five minutes when my desire to help Dave was put in real jeopardy. Father Bach was in full regalia, a brown cassock adorned with a rope-like belt and a heavy cross. I didn't like him right away. My association was with the Catholic Church, which I had always seen as hierarchical, not conceiving of the parishioners as in any way equal to the clergy.

A rotund, serious man with what I perceived as an imperious, patronizing demeanor addressed me: "Jane, you realize that you will be a

81

very important part of Dave's ministry, but I see here that you are not an Episcopalian. You will, of course, convert."

I didn't like his peremptory tone. 'You will, *of course,* convert.' My internal response was: *I am already a Protestant Christian by birth for God's sake. Isn't that enough?*

"Isn't Episcopalian a form of Protestant Christianity?" I asked demurely. "Can't I have my childhood minister from my Congregational church in Arlington, Massachusetts send a Letter of Transfer?"

"Oh no. You will need to take classes!" *Why do I need to take classes? I am not going to be a priestess. This is Dave's job, not mine.* He didn't explain why a Letter of Transfer wouldn't suffice. He simply told me what I must do. I felt my question deserved an explanation, not a proscription.

Evidently the mid-western diocese of the Episcopal Church was more in the papal tradition than the Episcopal churches I had known in the Boston area. The latter had displayed a distinctly Puritan influence at least regarding their elimination of anything suggestive of Roman Catholicism. Father Bach's church required catechism classes of me. My Catholic friends in Arlington all attended those, but I was raised with a healthy Protestant disdain for the papist church and its indoctrination of people through catechism classes. Then there was his title: "Father." This man came up to my chin. No Protestant clergyman I had ever known— not even the ones who were taller than I—insisted I call them "Father." We called them "Mister," like any other man.

With difficulty I held my tongue throughout the interview, acting as courteously as possible. I sat quietly, nodding agreeably at the appropriate moments and in no way revealing my irritation at what felt like arrogance towards me. By the time we emerged from the church offices to walk to our car I was seething. I could control my indignation no longer.

I hissed: "So, Dave, if you become an Episcopal minister, will I have to call you '*Father* Barry'?"

We were walking side by side. He was facing forward, but his eyeballs had rotated to peer at me. I sensed his sheepish grin in his response: "I guess so, honey—but only in public."

My retort burst forth without censorship: "Well, in that case FATHER Barry, you can just call me 'Mother Fucker,' but only in public!"

He guffawed, never one to reject a witticism, and then at the expiration of his laughter: "Oh! I guess this isn't going to work!" He never really had a calling anyway. He was simply trying to find a respectable, somewhat meaningful career path given the end of the university level academic road.

Needless to say, if Dave wasn't exactly suited to the clerical life, neither did the spouse of an Episcopal priest seem like a workable option for this would-be "liberated" wife. The handwriting was on the wall. Dave took a part-time, temporary position teaching history at a University of Wisconsin system community college campus.

During our Ph.D. studies—in an act of bravado—I wondered if I would ever actually make good on the threat—I had boldly declared that I didn't want to bear a child unless Dave agreed to be equally responsible for its care. Dave had agreed. So, as I finished my dissertation in 1975, our oldest daughter, Neville Morgan Barry, was born. For the first year of Neville's life, Dave and I shared childcare as I taught business English at night and he taught history daily at the community college. When his temporary academic appointment ended and I had decided to leave my low paying teaching job, there were no other opportunities for either of us in academia. He decided to try his hand at insurance and I agreed to stay home while studying for the real estate broker's exam. We were following the conventional path. Dave went out to work every day in the business world. I 'woman-ed' the home front. Tensions mounted as I found the home stifling and Dave hated business. We both complained. Finally, during an argument, we both agreed that we thought we could perform the other one's role better! So, we entered unchartered waters:

role reversal. He became a househusband, responsible for the house and the child and I went out into the marketplace as a real estate broker. In retrospect, I realize that we were pioneers doing this.

CHAPTER 10

Before Neville was born, we had moved to a fashionable area adjacent to Madison, Wisconsin called Maple Bluff, a picturesque neighborhood situated on a promontory overlooking Lake Mendota and the city of Madison. The sugar maples gave it its name and attracted us, especially in the fall when their vibrant color was a nostalgic reminder of New England. Despite the conventional constituency of our neighborhood, (most of the couples consisted of husbands who were corporate executives or professionals and wives who were homemakers), and our unusual role-reversed relationship, we were, curiously, socially accepted, and actually embraced by the power crowd. It seemed we were viewed as intriguing, young oddities, even 'avant-garde'—so long as we lived our own private lives without proselytizing the joys of the gender equal lifestyle. Thus, though we had a sociologically unusual household, we still had our niche in the mainstream. Our social life was active. Now, we, as a couple, were the "exceptions" who provided color and interest, perhaps even testimony to the open-mindedness of the people in an otherwise highly conventional community.

For our first 7 years in Maple Bluff, I felt that I had it all: not simply a professional life, but true equality with men as well—without sacrificing popularity and social acceptance. As a successful real estate broker working for a local Madison agency, I believed that I had equality with the opposite sex professionally and economically, and yet I also had the traditional blessings of a family and social acceptance in Maple Bluff. I went to the office every morning when Neville left for pre-school and then grammar school. Dave was there to greet her if I had to stay at the office or was otherwise engaged when she returned. Neville had playmates in the neighborhood. Dave and I had an active social life at the local country club, playing tennis with other members, going to cocktail parties.

By 1982, when I gave birth to our second daughter, Lydia, Dave and I had worked out a daily rhythm. He had assumed the position of primary caregiver to Neville and now, Lydia, as well as chief cook.

The real estate business can be 24/7 unless you set your own limits. People call at all hours. When I began in the business, if I got a call from a client before or during dinner, I would take it and often be absent from the table for the duration of a meal. That presented a real issue between the cook and me. Whereas we women often "keep the dinner warm" for our husbands, Dave, being a man, would have none of that. He demanded that the whole family be at the dinner table if he were going to make the dinner. So, the dinner hour became a sacrosanct time in our household, a time when we could count on everyone's being there and in those days 'sans' cell phones and texting.

I spent 6 mornings a week in the office working as a realtor and as many nights as was necessary with clients, more in the spring and summers than in the winter and fall. When I was showing houses at times that Lydia needed to be nursed, Dave would meet me on the road with her in tow. I would take a "coffee break" or a lunch break to nurse her and eat my own lunch. When that was accomplished, Dave took the baby home and I continued on my showing tour. It worked well.

Life wasn't exactly perfect though. We had our tensions caused by the role-reversed lifestyle. Dave was anything but meticulous. He didn't ever think that the furniture needed dusting, the carpets needed to be vacuumed or the beds changed despite clear evidence to the contrary. What I considered a mess, he considered life well lived. If I complained, he suggested that it was my problem for being "such a perfectionist." The solution was hired cleaning help; so, we hired a *cleaning gentleman.*

There was also the issue of the girls' clothes. While I loved fashion and wanted my girls to look a certain way, he was only concerned with getting something, *anything*, on them. One incident best summarizes our problem. I had shopped at a factory outlet for designer, Florence Eismann's, children's fashions, and bought some adorable, color coordinated summer outfits for the girls. The next day I arrived at the neighborhood club pool prepared to enjoy the spectacle of my daughters smartly dressed in their new outfits. Instead Lydia ran to greet me dressed in her stylish bathing suit and coverup but wearing red vinyl galoshes. When I recoiled in horror, interrogating Dave as to the reason for this grotesque fashion 'faux pas,' he explained matter-of-factly that he couldn't find her sandals. Whereas I would not have left the house until I found the damn sandals, he considered that effort a waste of time. When I complained, he said: "If you don't like the way they are dressed, you'll just have to be there to dress them." Not an option. So, I accepted the situation as it was, grateful that the girls had a wonderful parent caring for them despite his lack of fashion acumen.

Role reversal presented other interesting experiences. For instance, there was the time when Neville came running into our room one morning yelling: "Mom, Dad! The Tooth fairy brought me a dollar! He brought me a whole dollar!" Dave and I looked at each other surprised by the pronoun, 'he.' Dave queried her: "Neville, how do you know the tooth fairy is a man?"

"Easy! I saw his shoe. It's a man's shoe. Just like yours, Dad."

She obviously had no problem conceiving of the Tooth fairy as a *man*! We asked ourselves what in the world were we creating by our role-reversal?

Sometimes my hectic business schedule created chaos that wasn't usual for a wife and mother. One such event occurred when Dave and I were honored by an invitation to a formal dinner party by a very prominent Maple Bluff couple whose home was located next to the Governor's mansion. That day I was planning to leave work early but late in the afternoon a client called asking to make an offer on a property I had shown him the day before. I looked at the clock, 3PM. "If you come over to the office right now, I can do it." Well, the offer turned out to be more complicated than I anticipated and before I knew it, it was 5:45PM, 15 minutes after we were due at the dinner party. I rushed home to find Dave, the househusband, already gone and the babysitter in charge of Neville and Lydia. Neville followed me up the stairs as I stripped down trying to explain to her that I couldn't talk, that I was late, pulling on my dress sans underwear, changing shoes, no nylons.

"Aren't you going to put on some underpants, Mom?"

"Can't! I'm late. Be good, honey. I'll see you later."

Then, feeling guilty, not about the underwear, but rather for not paying attention to my daughter, I ran down the stairs and out the door. On my way to the party, I combed my hair and applied lipstick. Gathering myself, I knocked on the host's door, whereupon a maid, complete in black uniform with white ruffled apron, opened the door and pointed down a long hallway to a huge dining room where the 20 or so other guests had already taken their assigned seats. As I entered, the hostess seated directly across the table, cordially with subtlety indicated the one empty seat. Taking it, I introduced myself to the gentleman to my right saying, "Hi, Jane Barry." He gave his name. I smiled. Then, I turned to my left and stopped short because I realized that I knew the man but couldn't come up with his name on the spot. He was a portly, jowly, gray haired man.

I said, "Hi, I'm Jane Barry. I know you. Don't I?" Everyone at the table stopped talking and looked over with amusement.

"Why you probably recognize me because I am the Governor."

It was Lee Dreyfuss, the Governor of the state of Wisconsin, who was always recognizable because he never left home without sporting his red vest.

*

Initially when I went into real estate I worked for a firm across town, but not too long after, a neighbor who owned his own firm right on the border of Maple Bluff, recruited me to work for him. Given our burgeoning family, the location just minutes from our house was a welcome convenience.

Until that point, one of the larger Madison companies had dominated our neighborhood's real estate market. When my neighbor recruited me, we agreed that we would join forces to enhance our chances against the large firm. I was hired as his "Maple Bluff person," the one to whom he would refer any and all business in our affluent suburb.

One day, I arrived at the office jubilant because I had a wonderful new listing in Maple Bluff. The owner had been marketing the property in the local papers himself for a few weeks hoping to sell it FSBO (for sale by owner) to avoid paying any real estate commission, but the previous evening he had called me to ask me to list it. When I delivered the paperwork for the new listing to Dick, my broker, incredibly, he had a look of consternation.

"Jane, this listing was a FSBO in the paper and I assigned it to Vonda to pursue. I'm afraid that you will have to share this listing with her."

A common source of business for real estate agents was the newspaper classified ads. Agents often call sellers who have advertised their homes for sale to offer them real estate brokerage services. Dick, a hands-on, micro-manager, had assigned his secretary to comb the newspapers for FSBO's, which he then assigned to us agents to pursue. Most agents are perfectly capable of searching the newspapers themselves, but Dick ran a particularly paternalistic company where despite the fact that we, real estate agents, were not actual "employees" but instead were independent contractors responsible for generating our own business, he assigned and oversaw our work. Evidently, he momentarily forgot that he had agreed to refer all Maple Bluff business to me. By mistake he had assigned a Maple Bluff seller to another person in the office.

When he first said that I should share my listing, I did what was my habit: I simply nodded, remained mute and left his office. I was completely unprepared for what seemed to me such an outrageous violation of our agreement. I knew I had to protest because instinctively I knew his proscribed solution was unjust, but I wanted to develop my argument and hopefully, propose a logical and fair solution.

When properties that were listed with our company sold, the agent who secured the listing on the property got 50% of the listing side of the commission paid by the seller; the company got the other 50%. My broker wanted me to share *my* 50% equally with the other sales associate who had done nothing but receive an assignment from the boss. Back in my office, alone thinking, I reasoned that since he felt that he had some obligation to the other sales associate because he mistakenly assigned her to pursue the Maple Bluff property that I had listed, he could just as easily resolve the dilemma by sharing his *company's* half of the listing commission with her. I had done nothing wrong. I had pursued and secured a Maple Bluff listing, my assigned role in his company. He, on the other hand, had violated our agreement to refer any and all Maple Bluff leads to me. Now, he wanted me to resolve his problem with my share of the commission. Not right!

I went to see him. He was at the other end of the long narrow room which served as his office, seated behind a desk so mammoth, it occurred to me that he looked like a little kid playing grown up. As I approached him, I felt imposing. I was 5 foot 6 inches in stocking feet, but I was wearing my 3-inch business heels. I delivered the response I had been rehearsing:

"Dick, I've been thinking about the situation regarding Vonda. I understand that you feel she deserves payment because you assigned her the FSBO to pursue, but frankly, I feel that your solution is unfair to me. It was *you* who involved her against your promise to me that you would refer any and all Maple Bluff business to me. If anyone should share a commission with Vonda, it should be *you*, not me."

Suddenly his face lost its color, his brow furrowed and his eyes narrowed into a steely stare. He had a bass for a voice and it boomed:

"Jane Barry, I certainly am sorry you feel that way, but you are the one who will share your commission."

He was livid that I had the audacity to question his authority, something he wouldn't tolerate. But I was not about to share a listing commission I had earned by myself with no help from him or anyone else. I knew that if I hadn't listed that property, his company would not have secured the listing. The seller would have given it to the big company, our major competitor. The sole reason the seller listed with Dick's local company was because of me. He knew me as his Realtor neighbor. If I quit my job with Dick, the seller would withdraw the listing from his company. I was certain of that.

I took a deep breath and responded: "Dick, since that's the way you feel, I resign."

At the time I had about $15,000 worth of business pending, a relatively substantial percentage of my annual income. All the work had been done for each transaction. Only the actual closings remained to be executed before I would be paid. Since I was leaving before the closing dates, I wondered if Dick would pay me for my work.

For several weeks after the closings, I received no money. Whenever I called his office, I heard the classic: "The check's in the mail," but, of course, I never received any checks. To my chagrin I discovered that none of the State funded real estate regulatory boards, nor any of the professional organizations to which I belonged, had any jurisdiction over commission disputes between brokers and their agents. My only formal recourse to recover the withheld earnings was to file a civil suit. If I did that—with no assurance I would win—I would surely incur attorney's fees equal to or in excess of the commissions I sought to recover. I had done all the work; yet, I feared I might not get paid for any of it simply because I had objected to my broker's breaking our verbal contract, then unilaterally appropriating commissions I earned.

Since my only conventional option was a lawsuit, I decided to attack the problem unconventionally. I decided to hold a sit-in. Since I was a smoker at the time, I bought myself a new pack of cigarettes for the long haul, made sure I had plenty of matches and chewing gum and knocked on his office door. In response to the order to "Come in!" I entered to find him sitting as usual behind his huge desk at the far end of the room. I took a seat opposite him and began:

"Dick, I've been waiting for a couple of months now for my checks to arrive in the mail. As you know, that's never happened. So, I'm here, you're here; the checkbook is here. Please start writing so that I can be on my way."

"Jane, I have not written the checks; I don't intend to write the checks and I certainly am not going to be forced into writing them by you. You'd better leave now."

I held my ground. I had nothing to lose.

"I don't intend to leave without my earnings, Dick."

With that I reached into my purse for a cigarette, lit up and settled back for the long haul. Perplexed what to do with me and unable to do his own work with me sitting opposite him, staring at him and polluting his office with my smoke, he got up and walked out the door leaving his office to me.

For about a half hour I sat there wondering how things were going in the reception area where I was sure he was fussing with his receptionist. Soon, there was a knock at the door and before I could respond, two uniformed police officers entered. Being a regular at the local donut shop where they take their breaks, I was acquainted with them both. They had slight smirks on their faces suggesting that they saw the humor in the situation. Politely, they informed me that they must escort me out since I was trespassing on private property. I recognized that resisting would be futile.

My sit-in had failed to affect the desired payment, but it had given me an idea. Since my broker had chosen to call the police rather than deal with me, I decided to let the police know how Dick had been behaving— that in effect, he had stolen money he owed me. I knew he wouldn't be pleased for others to know that he wasn't paying one of his agents. Then it occurred to me that I should let *everyone* know.

Dick had been making his move socially in Maple Bluff. He recently had moved to a large home in the Village where his new neighbors were many of the respected elders of our tony, little community. One of these new neighbors, was an acquaintance of mine who was a Dartmouth alum and used to date women at Smith, affording a bond between us. He was a partner in a prestigious, old-line law firm. Conveniently, he lived directly across the street from Dick's new house. As soon as I left Dick's office, I hired that very attorney to write a letter to Dick on my behalf, in essence calling him a "dead beat" for not paying me the money I had earned. I knew the effect that this attorney's letterhead would have on him. Then, I went up to the country club where Dick and I both belonged and began telling anyone I met exactly what Dick was doing to me.

The next day a check for the full amount was in my mailbox—hand delivered.

CHAPTER 11

Having resigned from Dick's company I decided to join a "100% firm," that is a firm where the agents earn the bulk of the commission paid by the seller or the buyer, but are responsible for all their own marketing costs, costs which are usually paid for by a conventional brokerage firm. This type of arrangement only works for seasoned agents who feel confident they can rely on business from their own established clientele. By this time, I was that kind of agent.

In the spring of 1983 Dave and I were celebrating our 15th wedding anniversary. The day before we were to leave on a tour of New England bed and breakfast inns, I received a call from my neighbor to whom I had recently sold a home. The husband was being transferred and wanted to list the house for sale immediately. I was busy tying up loose ends of business before my vacation. Since another realty company had owned the home when I sold it to them and since that company still held the mortgage, I suggested that my neighbor try to work a deal on the commission by listing with that real estate company instead of with me. When the other company refused to cooperate, I was surprised. I thought they had forsaken an opportunity to list a nice piece of property. Because they wouldn't work with my neighbor, he again requested that I sell the house for him. I hurried to get the property on the market before leaving for my vacation.

Concerned that while I was away the other company might reconsider their hasty decision and try to abrogate my listing, I informed my Broker what had transpired. I let him know that my listing contract was legal and binding; that I had given the other company ample opportunity to list the property, but that they had declined. I provided my broker with a detailed itinerary of my trip and told him to be sure to contact me if there was any attempt by the other company to interfere with my listing.

When I arrived home from my vacation, a young couple was peering in the windows of the listed home. At their request I showed them the property and they wrote a full-price offer. Excited, I called the office to let them know the property had an offer. At this point the secretary informed me that my listing had been cancelled several days before. I was no longer the listing agent, no longer entitled to any of the listing side of the commission. I was incredulous. There had been no call from Tom regarding any attempt by the competition to nullify my listing. I said: "Are you sure, Carol? My sign is still on the property."

"Well, Jane, I don't know about that. I just know that Tom told me to take it out of our inventory, that Ace Realty now has that listing."

"WWWHATT?! Are you sure?" Then before she could say a word, I interrupted: "Carol, is Tom there? I'd like to speak to him."

My heart was pounding in my ears. *Can he actually have given my completely legitimate listing to Ace Realty without so much as discussing it with me when I had apprised him of the situation and specifically told him to call me?*

Suddenly, there were the honey tones, the verbal glad hand of Tom on the other end of the line:

"Hi Beautiful! Did you have a nice vacation?"

This was Tom's usual salutation to me. He was a stocky, balding, man of about my same age, and he seemed to revel in his repartee with me in which he always made note of his appreciation of my good looks. I usually played along, but not now.

"Tom, Carol just informed me that my listing has been transferred to Ace Realty! I specifically told you to call me if there was any attempt by them to take that listing! It was a completely legitimate listing! Why didn't you call me?"

"I know, Jane, but I made the decision to honor Ace's request. I just thought that you, being pregnant and all, needed a vacation without the disruption of business concerns."

It was true. I was pregnant with my third child, and the vacation from business concerns was nice, but we were talking about my living. When I wrote the offer on my own listing, I stood to earn $18,000, the whole commission, both the listing and the selling sides, money that would provide a financial cushion during my maternity leave. Now that he had unilaterally canceled my listing, I would lose $9,000, or half of the commission even though I would still receive the sale side because of the offer I had written. Ironically, Tom was assuming a fatherly, protective stance in view of my "delicate condition", treating me like a child, dismissing my real adult interests, to do what was convenient for him. He had totally ignored my explicit instruction to contact me if the other company prevailed upon him to release the listing. He didn't give any consideration to the fact that money was even more critical to me now because of my pregnancy. Soon we would have another mouth to feed while I recovered from childbirth. *We need that money!* I was outraged.

"Well, Tom, I cannot believe that you decided to give up my listing without so much as picking up the phone and calling me! I'm shocked. How dare you?" I hung up on him.

The listing was gone and I was sure that the other company would not just hand it back. My only chance at reclaiming my lost earnings was to appeal to my company's board to compensate me for the broker's outrageous action, but I knew the board would not be inclined to impugn his decision since it would mean paying me the $9,000, my agent's share of a listing commission the company would no longer be receiving from the seller. They might appreciate my outrage at my lost monies, but I would need to compel them to pay me. I explained this to Dave as we discussed my options.

"Well, I can see you are distressed at the turn of events," Dave said, "but on what basis can you persuade the board to rectify the situation? I mean you've said that once an agent like you gets a listing, the listing becomes the legal property of the brokerage firm, not your property. They have a right to do with it as they wish...right?"

"Yes, but I've been in the real estate business for 10 years and I have NEVER seen a company willingly turn over a high-priced listing, or *any* listing for that matter, to another company...and do it without so much as a call to the agent who listed it! I mean the other company might reconsider and want the listing they declined, but there was no reason to give it to them. I had done more than most agents would to make the listing available to them and they had refused it! Only then did I list the house at the seller's request. You would think that having been informed of the circumstances and of my assurance that it was a completely legal and binding listing, that Tom would either have rejected Ace's appeal for the listing or at the very least have discussed the matter with me...especially, since I told him to call me!"

Like a therapist, Dave looked over at me as I hyperventilated and he calmly, judiciously said: "So you feel devalued because you were not taken seriously, but instead, ignored."

I exploded at him: "Well, of course I do! Wouldn't you?!"

Again calmly: "Why do you think that Tom did this, Jane? Does he have a grudge against you?"

That was the question: *Why?* "Uh...nooooo...I don't think that he has a grudge against me."

In fact, we'd always had a more than cordial relationship.

I continued: "What I think happened was that Ace Realty reconsidered their decision and decided they wanted the listing once they saw the nice job I had done of marketing it online. They called Tom and asked for it. Probably because they are one of the biggest, most influential real estate companies around with an owner who is politically well connected, Tom acquiesced. He knew I wanted him to call me, but he probably wanted to avoid bad blood with Ace and figured he could sweet talk me. That's what he was trying to do when he told me that he was just being considerate of my 'delicate condition' by not bothering me while I was on vacation."

Dave latched right on to my phrase 'sweet talk.' "Do you think that he would have felt that he could 'sweet talk' any of the guys in the company?" The company was overwhelmingly male.

I was becoming exasperated: "Of course not! And none of them would be pregnant either!"

"That's not what I'm asking, Jane. You told him to call you. He ignored your directive. You feel devalued, ignored, dismissed. I am asking you if you think that he would have given away a lucrative, highly desirable listing in an upscale neighborhood if the listing agent had been one of the guys in the firm who had specifically told him to call if there was any move by the other company?"

I was writhing. My relationship with the men in my office had always been relaxed and fun. There had even been a certain amount of playful, sexual innuendo, particularly from Tom, the manager. I had considered it all in good fun and felt unthreatened. In fact, the situation had been comfortable for me because it was familiar. It incorporated my two identities as conformist, conventional female and exception. *I am a cheerleader, popular, friendly, attractive—traditionally feminine as evidenced by the banter—yet still effective as a businesswoman.*

But Dave was asking the acid question, the question I didn't want to ask myself: "Jane, do you think that Tom would have behaved the same if your name had been John?"

Immediately, I responded: "No...NO, I DON'T." I honestly couldn't picture Tom unilaterally voiding one of the male associates' most lucrative listing contracts, a plum of a listing, without at least discussing the matter with him—but my anger was not directed toward Tom. *I'm angry at Dave! I don't want to face this question or the answer.*

What do they say about the messenger? Well, at that moment, I could have killed Dave. He was making my life miserable. Now I had to deal with my consciousness that this incident would not have occurred if I were a male. I had to face the unpalatable truth that as a woman I hadn't been treated with dignity; that my opinions weren't worthy of attention; that Tom felt that I could be ignored with impunity. The manager knew the men in the company wouldn't tolerate such conduct, but his money was on my passive acceptance of my fate. Dave was sharing his knowledge of patriarchy. As a man he knew how men think. I was forced to accept the truth. Even if I appreciated his sharing his first-hand knowledge, it was painful to hear. It put me in the unwelcome position of having either to confront discrimination and lose male approval or be the wimp that Tom expected and lose my self-respect.

Tom's bet against me almost paid off. Despite the anger and indignity I felt at the lost commission, I really didn't want to confront the Board of Directors of my firm. I especially didn't want to declare their action "sexist," something I knew I had to do to right the wrong because listings were company's property, which they have the right to release to anyone—unless they are discriminating by doing so. To declare the act discriminatory meant transforming the situation from the product of an unintentional oversight or lapse—like the one with my former Broker, Dick—to the product of a sexist attitude. This accusation would pit me against all the men in our small, predominantly male company even if I didn't mean to include them all. If I charged sexism I figured the men would rally against me, considering the charge a personal affront or at the least considering me a dangerous bitch.

To contemplate ostracism from my male colleagues when I had been raised learning all the techniques to acquire male approval, when male approval had always been the name of the game, was terrifying. It threatened my very being, my gender identity, my view of myself as an attractive and desirable female. *In my eyes, male opinion was the priority.*

I saw myself as males saw me. My opinion of myself wasn't my opinion, it was male opinion. I had no worthy opinion. Male opinion was the important opinion.

It wasn't that I was romantically inclined toward any of my male colleagues and therefore wanted their approval—I wasn't—but their *disapproval* of me seemed more important than I could ever have imagined. Although I saw my stand as justifiable, although I believed the charge of sexism was deserved in this case, condemnation by the opposite sex was such a thoroughly traumatic prospect, I wanted to back down. My desire for male approval—my terror at its loss—was almost irresistible.

For my appeal to the board I hired an attorney to provide legal authority for my position that acquiescence to the other company's demand to void my listing contract was, in fact, strictly voluntary on my company's part—politically expedient to be sure, but legally unnecessary and ultimately, discriminatory against me. Hiring an attorney was a huge step for me. It meant I was serious; it meant I was assuming an adversarial posture, an adult confrontational, feminist posture. I was not appearing at the board meeting simply as a supplicant, looking for grace. I had already failed in my verbal request that the company management voluntarily rectify the situation. Now I was marshaling the legal facts to force them to correct the injustice.

Until now, circumstances and my own denial and avoidance tactics had always conspired to allow me to believe that I, personally, could defeat or avoid sexism, without a fight—amicably; that if there was a confrontation, it could be addressed personally and not ideologically. Charging the company with sexism using an attorney would change all that. I would lose that part of my identity, which made me acceptable to the power structure and therefore acceptable to my self-concept, my willingness to ignore, overlook, deny, minimize sexism even when it was blatant.

But this situation was outrageous.

As I prepared my statement for the hearing before the company board,

I discovered that whenever I even contemplated mentioning the word "sexism," I saw myself as breaking a code of silence and willful ignorance to which I had unwittingly subscribed. It felt as if I were violating a sacred, unwritten oath, breaking an unwritten taboo and in the process, becoming a "raving feminist", a troublemaker. Just the utterance of the word seemed heretical, revolutionary, because it implied knowledge of something I shouldn't know exists—except in the abstract or in other contexts...not in a context in which I was involved! It suggested a negative opinion of all men, which I didn't have.

A voice within chided me: "Only raving feminists make accusations of sexism—EVER." It was my mother's voice. This came from a hitherto forgotten, unacknowledged part of me that considered those accusations irrational and unfounded; the feminists who make such charges hysterical, emotionally unhinged. The inner conflict was all but paralyzing.

Even when I managed to overcome my own doubts about the validity of my perceptions and consciously acknowledge that Tom would NEVER have done this to me if my name were John, there was the obstacle of my sensation that by acknowledging sexism's existence and charging them with sexism I was committing treason. I was calling attention to a system of subordination of women and promotion of men that I had subconsciously learned—even in my own birth family—to accept in silence, even to deny its existence.

To label the company's action sexist also required acknowledging privately and admitting publicly that the comradery, the office "equality" in which I took such personal pride, had been illusory. It required facing the fact that I was not an equal member of the group, forsaking the illusion of my equality that allowed me to ignore sexist treatment. That was humiliating, embarrassing and painful. It was something I, who had always considered herself an exception to female inferiority and subordination, didn't want to admit.

I had the choice to say the ugly truth that I as a woman, better educated than most of the men in the firm, had not been regarded or treated as an equal and perhaps get my money back; or, I could keep silent, trying to preserve the charade of equality but lose my earnings. The choice was painful and frightening, but I made it.

Even though I still wanted to see my situation as an isolated case of miscommunication and appeal for a refund purely on the basis that my listing contract was enforceable and need not have been voided, I knew that was not true and without publicly declaring the truth—that this would never have happened to one of the males in the company...that the act was discriminatory—the Broker would stand on his right to control the listing and I would remain a financial victim. I would never see the $9,000 I earned. I steeled myself to go to the board meeting and blaspheme by using the awful "S" word publicly.

Before the meeting I sought out the sanctuary of one of the lady's room stalls nervously reviewing the notes I had painstakingly prepared for the occasion. I knew that if I didn't know the outline of my argument cold, my nerves would erase from my memory the points I wanted to make. My hands were clammy, my stomach queasy. I felt so tight, so brittle, I had the feeling that if I moved any part of my body precipitously, that part would crack and break off.

When I arrived at the meeting, the full board was assembled—one woman and approximately six men. After announcing that I had requested a hearing, the company manager turned the meeting over to me. I had written my remarks in a stiff notebook to avoid holding single sheets of paper that would reveal my involuntary trembling. Initially when I spoke, the volume of my own voice startled me. All I could think was: *That's your voice. It's so loud...TOO loud!*

I was terrified by its sound. By the third sentence I was quivering. My throat was going dry, my voice was faltering, my eyes riveted to my notes were smarting, making it difficult to see the type and I felt hot all over. *I'm not going to make it through this speech! But I've got to! This is much worse than my defense of my Ph.D. thesis!* Fumbling for my water glass, I took a sip, swallowed hard, took a deep breath and persisted, reading one word after another, unaware of what I was saying—simply trying to utter the syllables. After what felt like forever, the inner panic suddenly and miraculously subsided. I began to hear the words that I was speaking and was able to concentrate on the logic of my argument rather than on the terror of the occasion.

By the end of my speech when I raised the issue of the sexist attitude implicit in the decision to forsake my listing without so much as a phone call to me, the listing agent, I was on a roll. I looked up from my notebook, surveyed the room and came as close to eloquence as I am able. In that five-minute address I had taken a giant step on the emotional journey from daughterhood to adulthood. Despite the blasphemy, literally the 'breaking of silence,' I was still alive...more alive!

There was a "question and answer" period after I finished, which happened to incorporate some statements of opinion by board members on the matter at hand. To my surprise and delight a number of those present voiced agreement that I should be reimbursed the commission. Since the economic interest of all the board members was in direct conflict with mine, I was buoyed, but I didn't know what to expect when they adjourned to deliberate.

The deliberations took an interminable half hour. Minute by minute I vacillated between optimism and despair until they returned to announce that they had decided to reimburse me the full $9,000. I had stood up for myself, confronted the ugly truth that I had been the victim of sex discrimination and the board had agreed to repay me the money that they had deprived me. I did not tolerate their disrespect. I asserted my adult equality and re-claimed my self-conception as an exception to female subordination. I felt victorious and proud. It wasn't easy, but I did it. I left the office feeling like Super Woman!

The next morning when I arrived at the office, the usual banter had stopped. Tom was speaking to the secretary as I walked in:

"Hi Tom."

"Hi Jane."

No 'Hi Beautiful.' *What happened? Overnight I had lost my beauty? Well, I guess that's ok.* Actually, it was a relief not to have to waste time and energy pretending to like sexually tinged socializing with a guy who held no attraction for me, but it was an early indication of a distinctly different attitude toward me that evidenced itself daily. The fellows weren't overtly hostile, but they didn't stop by my desk for casual chit chat anymore and whenever there was a dirty joke, I was either not included or someone expressly remarked: "Better not tell that one in front of Jane." I was seen as different now, a changed person. Only serious conversations about business took place in front of me and even less of that. All intimacy was gone. I was truly an exception, at least in the sense that they wouldn't treat me differently from the men in financial matters, but I had lost my conventional female identity that I had always coveted and protected. *I can be an exception, treated like the men in a business context, but now I am officially a bitch as well.*

I was getting a dose of reality. I had thought that I was truly an equal in the office but I found out that I was self-deluding in order not to face the truth that they saw me as a woman, second class. To get equal treatment I had to confront their sexist attitude for what it was. Now, they were letting me know there was a price to pay for that. It was disappointing, but I accepted it. If lack of familiarity and friendliness was the price for me as a woman to get real respect and most importantly real respect from myself, I would pay it.

CHAPTER 12

In 1984, I had just given birth to our third daughter, Margaret, named after my mother. My parents were coming to Wisconsin to meet their new grandchild. Every other time they visited they'd stayed in an extra bedroom in our four-bedroom home. This time the only spare bed was a pullout couch in the family room, the "nerve center" of the house and the primary residence of our three hyperactive terriers. Since with the birth of our third child we were not only still in an adjustment period but also no longer had an extra bedroom, we felt that this time a hotel for my parents would be in order. As I contemplated this solution, I knew that my parents would consider this idea "wrong," but I decided that we needed the space, both physically and emotionally.

Given our budget constraints, I investigated a number of options, finally settling on a retreat house nearby—the St. Benedict's Center— which rented inexpensive suites. We engaged one overlooking Lake Mendota, consisting of a bedroom, a sitting room and a private bath. It was decorated simply, but was very clean, quiet and pleasantly bright with a breath-taking view of the capitol dome across the lake in downtown Madison, use of a private swimming pool and access to lovely walking trails.

Taking the path of least resistance, I decided to communicate this so-lution and my reasons for these accommodations by letter to my parents. I carefully explained that I needed as much privacy, rest and space as possible being only a month 'post-partum.' By writing instead of calling, I wouldn't have to introduce the subject of the accommodations in a forum which permitted immediate rebuttal, such as a telephone conversation.

I thought I was so smart until my father, who had never phoned me in the twenty years since I left my childhood home, called. Unnerved to hear his voice on the other end of the line and having conveniently repressed any memory of the letter about the St. Benedict's Center that I had just sent him, I immediately feared that something was terribly wrong at home with my mother. Close but not quite. Something was terribly wrong all right, but not with my mother. Something was wrong with *me!* Dad was apoplectic about the St. Benedict's accommodations.

At first, he controlled his anger saying simply: "Jane, I got your letter."

"You did?" *Whoops!...Ooooh dear...I forgot about that letter.*

"Jane, your mother and I would prefer to stay in your home."

"Dad, I know you feel that way, but with three children, two of them babies, three dogs, my full-time business and a nursing schedule still not totally regulated, the house will be too hectic with all of us here 24/7."

He could no longer control his anger.

"JANE, I AM NOT STAYING IN ANY GOD DAMN MONASTERY!"

Despite the fact that he was in Massachusetts and I was in Wisconsin, a thousand miles away; despite the fact that I was 38 years old, 17 years married, the mother of three children, a Ph.D. and a successful business woman—a "liberated woman" for God's sake—I was literally trembling with fear. What was I afraid of? I didn't really know, but I was so scared my kneecaps were quaking and I was feeling light-headed. I knew that I needed to summon the courage to resist the feeling that I should capitulate to and obey him. It was time for me to stand firm, time to grow up as I had been doing in other venues, but everything in me resisted. I blurted out the sentence I had been practicing incessantly for just such an occasion:

"Dad, I know you feel that way." I felt that I was being arrogant.

How can I be saying this to my father...that I know he feels that he wants to stay in my house...and then not capitulate to that desire...demand?

When I discussed my fear of my parents' reaction to the St. Benedict's accommodations with our therapist, he suggested this response of acknowledging his "feelings" would be non-combative, a simple statement of Dad's point of view without objecting or conceding to it. I had practiced saying this in my mind each time I envisioned this encounter. Still, it was a lot easier to say it in my imagination than aloud to my father—especially because he didn't seem to perceive it as non-combative! Instead, he was yelling that he would find his own damn place to stay if he couldn't stay at our house.

To this response, I didn't know *what* to say, so I simply repeated the exact same words a third time: "I know you feel that way," continuing in a bumbling sort of way: "But Dad, the night you and mom arrive is the Friday of homecoming week-end at the University of Wisconsin. The hotel space in Madison is scarce and at an extreme premium. The suite I got for you is by far the nicest available that we can afford."

I was trying to let him know that I recognized his feelings, but that circumstances were motivating me to have chosen this particular place, the "God damn monastery."

I was singularly unsuccessful in my appeal to the circumstances that necessitated the St. Benedict's Center. I could have booked him into the Ritz. The quality of the accommodations wasn't the issue. It was that he was not being accommodated in our home.

He peremptorily instructed me: "Jane, cancel those reservations right now. Your mother and I will find our own damn accommodations, THANK YOU." *I don't think my father has ever been so angry with me. Then again, I have never given him occasion to be.* "We'll take care of ourselves, THANK YOU." His tone was one I'd never experienced before—ice cold, bitter, sarcastic. The next thing I heard was click and the dial tone.

The message was clear. I was not "taking care of" my parents the way as *his daughter* I should. My parents had their standards of what is right and wrong behavior. This was definitely wrong behavior. Family always stays with family. They had a right to stay at our house. I was not honoring that right. That I was paying for the two weeks of accommodations was irrelevant and in no way mitigated "the sin". It may have even magnified it. When family stays with family there is no apparent financial cost, but if I put them up somewhere else, it is clear that someone else is paying for them if he isn't—a humiliation for my father. They didn't want to pay, but they didn't want to be beholden either. It was a matter of pride.

I certainly didn't want to offend or hurt them, but I had. It was clear. Of course, I loved them and wanted them to be happy. I particularly wanted them to share our joyful time with our newborn, Margaret, but I knew their habits. Mom tended to be a night owl; Dad, a morning person. If I didn't have some privacy, some down time, specifically some time at night in the house without kids and parents to finish up one day and plan the next, the pace of life would overwhelm me. I explained all this in my letter to them, but still my desire for privacy and my action to fulfill my desire felt like rejection to them—and sadly truth be told, to me as well.

When Dad said that they would 'prefer' to stay at our house rather than stay at a hotel, I perceived his preference as an order, telling me the way things should be. In my subconscious, Dad's "preferences" were supposed to be honored by me, even at 38. Somewhere deep in my being I knew that. Non-compliance, once he had expressed his will, was treachery. When I didn't comply, he exploded again. If I rejected him when I arranged for the hotel room, I was compounding my offense by resisting when he specifically repudiated my action. By resisting I was implicitly, but pointedly, rejecting his preeminence in my life. Even after I became an adult chronologically and until that moment, I was a daughter all of my life, subject to his will, not his equal.

I knew intellectually, that I needed to take care of myself and *my* family but this rupture with my father was very painful. I empathized with my parents' desire to stay with us, not simply from a financial point of view, but also from an emotional one, because we were family.

We loved each other. We used to live together, not just visit each other. Staying in a hotel seemed like a rejection of him as family even though I didn't mean it that way. He reacted angrily and I understood why. I had always wanted his approval, but if I were to honor the validity of my own judgment as an adult as to what was best for me and my family, Dave and our 3 daughters, I had to choose to act in a way that caused pain to, and disapproval from, my father.

As it happened, when Dad rejected the accommodations I arranged, he certainly didn't stay at any "GOD DAMN MONASTERY." In fact, instead, he and mom ended up renting a room overlooking a dingy stretch of busy highway at the Manalo Inn, a motel known around town to rent by the hour, the only accommodations he could find available on Homecoming Weekend in Madison, WI. Still, my mother supported Dad's anger, going so far as to compliment the place he had found by saying she met some "interesting people" there. No doubt.

*

My single most powerful ally during this time of conflict and stress with my father was Al-Anon, a program I initially resisted when a few years earlier Dave disclosed the unwelcome and totally unexpected news that he was struggling with alcoholism, the same disease that killed his father. We had initiated a cocktail hour before Neville was born. It was comprised of a vodka tonic each night before dinner. This wasn't something I was familiar with from my parents, but Dave's mother and stepfather always had a drink before dinner so we followed suit. One night out of the blue Dave said he wanted to discuss our cocktail hour. At that point he revealed his incipient addiction, saying that he thought that he had the genetic propensity because at the end of our nightly cocktail hour, 2 ounces each, he always craved more. This was the first I had any inkling of the problem, but we both agreed that the situation deserved medical attention. That led to outpatient treatment for both of us because as we learned, alcoholism is a family disease.

While I didn't appreciate it at the time, it was fortunate for us both that he confronted his disease early and proactively before friends, family or even I was aware of it. He not only spared our suffering, but he also offered me the benefit of the "affected family members" program. The thrust of that program is to encourage those living with the alcoholic to recognize the separateness of each individual from every other individual. The concept is called "detachment." Detachment doesn't mean disinterest, lack of concern, lack of love or lack of empathy for the alcoholic individual. Instead it means recognition that everyone is a separate person and that as such we have no control, nor should we have control, over others' lives. Everyone has a right to live his or her own life.

This concept helped me to recognize and embrace my own "separateness," to accept that I was a unique individual with my own separate, different and individual feelings, desires and beliefs and that this is natural and ok, not a rejection of anyone else. This idea of separateness felt heretical and revolutionary—difficult for me to entertain and accept, but if I was separate from my alcoholic husband, then I was separate from everyone else—my parents included. With this separateness came the opportunity, the permission, the challenge, to hear my own voice, to affirm myself even when in disagreement with my parents: in short, the separateness presented the challenge to grow up.

Through Al-Anon I heard about and participated in "The Wounded Child" seminar on the experience of children of alcoholics and other dysfunctional families. It was a viscerally painful weekend where each participant was encouraged to try to reach back in time to meet and talk to our young, child selves.

The leader of the seminar greeted us with the story of his own childhood growing up in an alcoholic household where frequently he was awoken in the middle of the night by his parents' raucous arguments about his father's alcoholism. In the morning, his mother would try to conceal the episode and re-establish order by portraying the fights as a bad dream the child had experienced in his sleep: an illusion, not reality. Because of his mother's well-meaning attempts to hide his father's alcoholism by reconstructing reality, for many years his faith in his own power of perception and judgment was undermined. His story mirrored my experience with Mom about Dad's epilepsy.

The seminar leader tasked us participants with writing a letter to our own wounded child, to parent and comfort her, as we would have liked to have been parented and comforted as children:

> *Dear Janie,*
>
> *I know how hard you are trying to be a good, little girl, to make your parents proud of you, to do exactly what they want you to do all the time: to be smart, to be pretty, to be popular, to be obedient, to be a good person. You really try hard. I know it's difficult and you are tired and scared you will not succeed in satisfying their expectations. You go to Church Fellowship meetings because your parents think that Fellowship is good for you. They are unaware that you feel disliked and ostracized by many of the girls there. You feel lonely there. You do your best to endure those times.*
>
> *When you go to the dentist, you bravely don't cry even when you're hurt and scared, because you want to make your mom proud of your courage. You want to be the strong, brave daughter she expects you to be.*
>
> *You work very hard in school not to make any mistakes, to get all A's, not to waste money, not to break or do anything that will cause extra expense for your family, not to do anything that will embarrass your parents.*

I want you to know, Janie, that it's ok if you make mistakes. It's ok if you cry when the dentist or doctor hurts you. I'm sad you have had to go to those Fellowship meetings where you feel disliked. I love you even if you don't or can't do these things. I love you just the way you are.

I emerged from the seminar emotionally exposed, vulnerable, raw, realizing that internally, my desire to be loved and approved of meant always doing what others, particularly my parents, wanted me to do. If my feelings or values differed from my parents', I saw mine as unworthy, wrong, selfish. As a "good girl," "a daughter all of my life," feelings, thoughts or activities which didn't accord with my parents' proscriptions were to be avoided and condemned. It was never necessary or even proper to have, or to be in touch with, my own feelings. On the contrary, I sensed that the way to be loved was to deny my own feelings when they conflicted with my parents'. Thus, my conundrum to answer when way back in 1970 Dr. Gilbert had asked me how I felt about the amount of time my parents were planning to stay for their first visit to Madison. When I actually *did* feel my own feelings, if I took action to attain my desires that conflicted with the desires of others, frequently I felt guilty, selfish. When I was tasked with empathizing with my child self, I realized that Janie was afraid that if she showed her real self, her real desires, and thoughts, she would not be loved.

Geographic distance and age had been irrelevant. In my subconscious my mother and father maintained ultimate authority over me well into my adulthood. In a way, I existed as a separate human being only to do their will. Of course, living in a different part of the country, every minute had not been spent obeying their specific orders. Ninety-nine percent of what I did, I did on my own—without their knowledge. But that didn't seem to matter. Their general authority over my life had remained intact in me for many years, deeply internalized, because I never before had openly asserted my own authority over my own life. I never challenged their authority. Until I did.

In this "monastery incident"—for the first time in my life—I was openly asserting my own will in my own life, even when it conflicted with Dad's. I had embraced my separate and personal point of view, one that despite my father's angry appeal to my daughterly duty would prevail in my home. This act was not easy. On the contrary, my father and mother's unhappiness at that time precipitated an epic battle inside me, but I was staying true to myself and in consciously breaking the filial convention of daughterly submission, I suddenly became cognizant of patriarchy everywhere. If I was no longer willing to have my own father call the shots for me, I certainly was not going to act the child with men who were no blood relation.

CHAPTER 13

Maple Bluff was the kind of place where the good weather buzzed with the unabated sound of landscape companies mowing lawns and trimming hedgerows; where on trash day the lords of the manors neatly arranged their refuse containers along the curb at the foot of their driveways like so many sentinels set to guard the lovely damsels during their absence; where it was possible to see personalized license plates on a husband's car which consisted of his initials followed by the roman numeral I, on the wife's car by *his* initials followed by the roman numeral II and subsequent roman numerals on the children's cars. Although by 1984 even Maple Bluff had a growing contingent of "working mothers," most of the women were not the primary wage earners. The men held the lucrative positions in local industry, business, government or the professions and many of the wives supported the garden club and a variety of volunteer organizations.

In short, Maple Bluff was unabashedly traditional, a male dominated world. I had been vaguely aware of the almost exclusively male domination of our local government but since I was not personally interested in politics or public office, the issue hadn't concerned me—not until one day in November of 1984.

When I left Tom's company earlier that year, I formed my own firm rather than affiliating with another company. This decision wasn't precipitous. Ever since Dick's insistence that I share my commission with the woman he had appointed to pursue the Maple Bluff FSBO, and Tom's donation of my listing to Ace Realty without consulting me, I had been considering such a move. Over the years I had gradually established a loyal clientele so there was the obvious benefit to self-employment of increased salary as well as complete autonomy—freedom from any further exposure to patronizing bosses. Still, to start my own business was intimidating. It meant being responsible for all decisions and, of course, risking failure. To escape subordination, I had to step out from under the umbrella of its protection. This step was the culmination of an emotional progression. Finally, I was willing to be my own boss, my own authority.

To minimize overhead I started by working out of the basement of our home so I was there on that fateful day when the mail arrived, bringing a letter from the village addressed personally to "Mr. David Barry." Curious why our village would be writing exclusively to Dave, I nevertheless resisted the urge to peek. Instead, I dutifully placed the letter on Dave's personal pile.

At dinner I raised the topic: "What was that letter to you from Village Hall, Dave?"

He looked puzzled. "What letter?"

"The one that I left for you on the front hall table that was addressed specifically to you."

"I don't remember getting any letter from the village...?" he said, perplexed. Then suddenly he thought he might know what I was referring to. "Oh! Do you mean "The Maple Bluff Bulletin?" he asked, skeptical that this could be the subject of my inquiry. His blasé tone suggested its insignificance to him.

Now I was really confused. *So, it's the newsletter, the monthly mailing that contains everything from trivia about garbage pick-up to such items of consequence as announcements of caucus meetings and elections, that arrived in that mysterious envelope?*

"Dave, does the bulletin always come in an envelope addressed only to you?" I was struck by the weirdness of that possibility. He realized why I was perplexed:

"Now that you mention it...yeah, I guess it does! Strange, huh?"

Dave and I both were approaching a moment of revelation, experiencing an epiphany. We'd lived in our house for 10 years without realizing

118

that the village communicated solely with him. *It must be a clerical error. Did the Village of Maple Bluff somehow mistakenly miss putting my name on its mailing list when we bought our house and moved into the village 10 years ago?*

After the kids and Dave went to bed, I was sitting by myself in the family room watching the television, thinking: *My name should be on the official mailing list. I am, after all, everything Dave is: a legal citizen, a resident of the village, a homeowner of record, a taxpayer. I am as much a part of our community as he is, at least as well known and well regarded as he.* I decided to honor my desire to be included as an equal by writing a letter to the Village President requesting that my name be included in any future correspondence.

As I was preparing to write on my note card, I heard my own thoughts:

You're being picky, Jane. Why do you have to have your name on the envelope? O.K. so your name was omitted. The next time mail comes from the village addressed solely to Dave, just recognize that it's really meant for both of you and open it. Chill out. Don't be so egotistical and needy. But, really, Dave has little, if any, interest in the details of village business! I'm the only one in the house who always conscientiously reads every village bulletin. But, if I press to get my name on the mailing list, won't I justifiably be considered demanding and egotistical? A bitch here in the village too?

Not wanting to seem hostile or threatening, I chose cutesy stationery, a card sporting a bullfrog on a lily pad. Not exactly formal or businesslike. While I wanted to be treated as an equal citizen with my husband, I also felt the need to present myself to my "village fathers" as non-confrontational and innocuous. I didn't want to be perceived as demanding, bitchy. I had recently opposed my father's will and been excoriated by him; I had insisted that I be respected and paid what I earned at Tom's company and been silently ostracized. Now, I wanted to avoid confrontation. I simply wanted to have my name included on the mailing list.

As I reviewed the note for tone and grammar, to make sure it was suitably ingratiating, a shocking thought occurred to me: *What if the absence of my name on the envelope isn't a clerical error? Could it be gender-related; could it, in fact, reflect general village policy? Oh my God, could it be that NO women are included on the village mailing list...?*

Suddenly my palms felt sweaty and I actually heard and felt my heart beating in my head! *Could this be a case of institutionalized, governmental sex discrimination? I've read about such a thing, but never been conscious of it in my own back yard—though maybe it's been there all the time.*

Of course, nothing had changed in Maple Bluff. The discrimination had been there ever since we took occupancy—and no doubt long before that—but before this moment I wasn't ready to see it or to acknowledge it. I saw what I wanted to see. For ten years I managed to miss the fact that it was addressed only to Dave.

I knew I had reached an invisible border. To proceed further, to say or do anything to call attention to the possible inequity, even to consider it or to call it an "inequity," meant crossing, again, into "forbidden" territory.

*

Dave was upstairs in bed. I wanted to get his take on this. *Am I paranoid or narcissistic to think that the fact that my name isn't on the envelope is evidence of a general situation and that it's important?*

Once again, I was facing the humiliating idea that my equal standing with men was illusory or at the most, superficial. In the earlier instance, I had faced into my fear of ostracism from a small group, the company board, declared the act sexist and taken action to recover my lost commissions. The company board wanted to hide the issue, not broadcast it. There was an important difference here though. I couldn't simply ask for personal justice—in effect, the token "exception" status I managed to extract from my company.

Here, it was clear that personal justice necessitated justice for all. What good would it do even me if I, one woman, were included on the mailing list? Without the other women's names on the mailing list, the presence of mine would be useless. Each man could be assured that every other man in the village was being notified of village business, but as a woman, I would not have that right if the other women were not informed. For the first time, I realized that actually attaining personal equality with the men was clearly not a simple matter of demanding to be treated as an individual exception to the rule of female subordination. It required confronting *the rule itself.* It had taken me twenty years to realize what my feminist Smith housemate was saying when she insisted that we unite to confront sex discrimination.

Significantly, I had never been able to understand the aphorism "A chain is only as strong as its weakest link." Somehow it had never made sense to me. It sure did then as I realized that even if I were successful in being treated as an equal to a man and sent the bulletin, the fact that I was a woman and that all the other women might remain excluded, adversely effected my political influence.

Why was I worrying about the egotism of requesting my name on the mailing list? If my suspicions were correct, I needed to highlight and challenge a whole discriminatory power structure. In asking whether women as a rule were excluded from the mailing list or whether this situation was the result of intention, of a policy, now that's a different story altogether. Those questions challenged the rule itself, the unstated, incredible, implicit premise that women were not necessary to the political process, nay that women didn't belong in the political process.

I added a paragraph to my letter: "Is it the policy that only the male adults at an address are sent village mail? If this is the case, I would like to see this policy changed. What, if anything, must I do to initiate this change?"

With that brief paragraph I was presuming to suggest that women were adults, too. I had finally reached the point where the uneasy balance, the schizophrenic co-existence between Jane, the woman who would be the equal with men, and Janie, the eternal daughter, who would be accepted by being an exception but not an agitator, would no longer work. I was not simply seeking accommodation as an exception to a rule I implicitly endorsed—at least for other women—no longer asking for a "privilege" like a child. Instead I was directly challenging the subordination of women as a group to men. I was rejecting the treatment of us all as "daughters all of our lives." This was necessary because, as I now realized, without equality for all women, my equal status was vulnerable...no, face it, unattainable.

Before I received the village President's response to my froggy notepaper letter not only had I confirmed that the mailing list was almost exclusively male, but another Maple Bluff Bulletin had arrived for Dave only, this one announcing the date and place of the 1985 annual caucus, the meeting held to nominate candidates for village offices. That caucus announcement contained a statement which totally incensed me: "It is important that we have a large, representative group of village voters attend the caucuses since they constitute our Primary Elections." I then realized that a very "large...group of village voters"—the women—who comprised over 50% of the electorate, were not being informed of these caucuses.

There were to be four vacancies on the board because the terms of the president and 3 trustees were expiring. Of course, the retirees were all men. The connection between the lack of notification of women and the absence of women in the village government was becoming clear to me.

The 'coup de grace' occurred when the real estate tax bill arrived addressed to both of us: David S. *and Jane M. Barry.*

First, I discovered that I was not being sent the bulletins; second, that almost no women in the village were on the mailing list and thus neither were they sent the bulletins; third that this meant that the village was not sending its female citizens voting information since that was communicated primarily through the bulletin and finally, fourth, that we women were being made equally responsible for the taxes and therefore for financing the very bulletins and electoral announcements we were not being sent. Having grown up in the Boston area, I imbibed with my tea the mantra of the Boston Tea Party, "Taxation without representation." In a very real sense we Maple Bluff women were experiencing just that: taxation without representation…at least without equal representation.

I immediately dashed off a second letter, this time in a formal, business format and on personal letterhead to the whole board raising the issue of the exclusion of women from the mailing list and stating that if they wanted a "large representative group" at the caucus, they ought to send the bulletin to such a group, that is, to women as well as to men. I further raised the issue of the legitimacy of any electoral results in which the females were not given the same notice as males. I stated that their omission of the women was "tantamount to stuffing the ballot box."

Given my apparently liberated status, a Ph.D. owning her own business, living a life of role-reversal, having challenged subordination both professionally and in my family, one might have predicted that such a challenge to sex discrimination in my municipality would be emotionally easy for me. It was anything but. It precipitated not only war "without," for it did pit me against the male board in the village, but more importantly it caused all-out war inside me. I fought against myself daily, against my own imbedded, subconscious view that women *were* relatively speaking, like children deserving of second-class status. I had no real confidence in my stand.

Until this point, I had said nothing to any of my friends or acquaintances in the village regarding the mailing list issue. I wanted to keep the whole thing under wraps. As a real estate broker, I knew that controversy was not good for business. I didn't want to erect any unnecessary obstacles to people listing their homes with me. That was a very practical reason for discretion, but not by any means the whole story. Truth be told, I didn't want to risk the disapproval of my fellow Maple Bluff women and men and I wasn't sure that it wasn't an insignificant issue; I had always seen the bulletin; it wasn't an earth-shaking situation that my name wasn't on the envelope.

Even if I told the other village women that their names were not there either, would they care? Or would they resent that I was involving them in an unnecessary controversy? I knew that I, personally, felt more comfortable, more justified, prosecuting the issue for the inclusion of all women on the mailing list than I did for myself alone, but still, would they see the need?

I decided to confide in a friend of mine. Revan was more than 10 years older than I and thus, was not raised in the era of women's lib. Betty Friedan hadn't even written *The Feminine Mystique* initiating the Second Wave of feminism until Revan was in her mid 20's. Her life had been more traditional; she was a boarding school girl, the daughter of a wealthy Wisconsin family. Bright, she graduated from an elite New England boarding school and went on to Cornell. No career followed. Instead she became a wife and mother, volunteering civically, playing tennis and golf, keeping a lovely home for a fellow Cornell grad, her husband, who was the breadwinner while she participated economically solely via her inheritance.

She recently had made an attempt to serve on the Village Board, having volunteered in the Village for a number of years. Her political bid met with near humiliating defeat so I thought she might be amenable to challenging the 'status quo.' And because she was friendly with many of the movers and shakers in the village, her support would be invaluable.

As I pulled up in front of her elegant, Tudor home situated on a prime lot on the Lake Mendota waterfront, I was nervous. I was ostensibly coming for a "cup of tea," but the real reason was to confide in her, to enlist her support, if only emotionally, for what I was attempting.

Revan answered the door dressed impeccably as usual. She might have been playing golf since she had on a white sleeveless polo shirt and navy Bermuda shorts. She and her home looked like something out of *Architectural Digest*. Everything was perfect from her well-coiffed hair to her newly renovated kitchen. I took a seat and a glass of iced tea, and we chatted for a few minutes about the renovations before I started in:

"Revan, I have something important to talk about. I need your take on something that I seem to have become involved in."

Until that moment, the most serious activity that we had ever shared was our attempts to quit smoking, at which we both succeeded. She was bustling around the kitchen putting the tea back in the fridge, cutting some fresh lemon. She stopped in her tracks to give me attention:

"Sure. What's going on?"

She was sincere and seemed to want to help...but then again, she didn't know what I wanted yet. If she did, she might not have been so solicitous.

"Have you heard anything about me and the village?" Since Revan was a long-term resident of Maple Bluff, a scion of a successful, Wisconsin family, and as such, embraced wholeheartedly, perhaps she had heard something.

Eyebrows knit, she replied: "About you? No...what are you talking about, Jane?"

"Well, I seem to have stumbled onto a...a...sexist situation in the village."

It was tough to get that "S" word out even when confiding in a friend. I was struggling with how to present my discovery. On the one hand, by my identifying or characterizing the exclusion of women from the mailing list as 'sexist,' not simply as an innocent or accidental omission, she would probably perceive me as a troublemaker. On the other hand, if I simply told her that I was trying to get women on the mailing list, she might consider the effort to do that misspent, gratuitous, of no real consequence. As I struggled to confide in order to get her help, I felt sad and frustrated that I was not confident enough in our relationship to trust that she wouldn't see me negatively. In fact, I feared that she would reject me altogether, that she would see me as weird, as my mother perceived me when I told her I was going to study for my Ph.D. I was afraid she would see me as literally eccentric, 'ex centro,' outside the circle. I didn't have confidence enough in her to know that she would see the mailing list situation for what it was.

"Revan, I have discovered that the village mailing list is almost completely male. Excuse the pun, but every living male resident and many dead men are on the mailing list, but there's hardly a woman."

Reflexively, she responded without a beat:

"REALLY?! I'm surprised by that!"

"Yes, it's true. And furthermore, I've realized...after living here *for ten years and* being oblivious...that the village bulletins and the announcements of caucus meetings and elections come only to Dave, but the tax bill that pays for everything comes to *both* Dave and me, making both of us financially responsible for them. That's taxation without representation, Revan—something that as a Massachusetts girl I grew up knowing that we, Americans, rejected at the Boston Tea Party!"

I was getting exercised as I told her about this. She seemed, in contrast, to grow more deliberative, taking in the information and trying to sift through it to decide how to react. There was a chasm developing between us. I felt it.

"Well...yes...that doesn't seem...uh, right. What have you done, Jane?"

Her response was measured now...none of the passion that I had been feeling ...and evincing none of the spontaneity of her first reaction. I thought she was becoming wary of danger. *She is probably wondering what the situation is with the Village Board, not wanting me to make a* scene. *Am I seeing this wrong? Still, I must test the waters.*

"Revan, I have sent two letters...one about 3 weeks ago to Patrick (the Village President) telling him to put my name on the mailing list...I had noticed that I wasn't on it and..."

"*YOU* aren't on it?" she interjected, just now registering this fact and obviously surprised and bewildered by it, given that I was well known in the village.

"No...but neither are YOU!"

"I'M NOT?!" Her surprise was genuine and not to be contained, but almost immediately, she tempered herself.

"Well...I ...I guess I never look at the envelope, but I know that I do read the bulletins."

"But that's not the point, Revan. The point is that you and I pay taxes! Somehow, we don't get treated the same as men. That's the point.!"

"...hmm."

No real response. Again, as I was becoming more exercised she was becoming more passive. Suddenly, she turned toward the fridge:

"Would you like some more iced tea, Jane?"

I was frustrated. "No. No thanks. But, Revan..."

I tried again....

"So how do you feel about this situation?" The question reminded me of Dr. Gilbert's, our therapist, querying me as to my feelings about the length of my parents' visit when I couldn't get in touch with my own feelings.

She wiped up some tea that she noticed on her new counter. "Well...it's not...right, but I mean I *do* see the bulletin so it's not really that big a deal. Is it? I mean, *practically* speaking? Don't you think that most women in the village are aware of what's going on here...that most of us see the bulletin when it comes? I know I do. Jane, I mean, I think it might be unnecessarily pushy for us to insist that the village revamp the whole mailing list ...just to get our names on it".

"Revan, imagine if I told you that Maple Bluff had experienced a computer meltdown and all 500 or so of the men living here, including your husband, would no longer be sent the bulletin, the main communication between our village government and its residents/citizens—that from now on only *we women* would be sent the bulletin. Further what if I told you that the men would continue to be taxed and held equally responsible for the village expenses. What would you think about that!?"

Immediately, she responded: "Oh, of course, I mean, it wouldn't be right!"

"Precisely! It wouldn't be! Well, that is exactly what's happening to us!"

Her brow knit again, her eyes expressing her consternation. She was being pressured, feeling uncomfortable.

"Well, Jane,...I see your point...so where do things stand?"

Just as I was about to fill her in on where things stood, her husband arrived home. He was in his 60's, a nice looking fellow, a club champion golfer who made his living as a wholesaler in metal.

"Hi Bill! How are you?"

"Hey, Jane! What's up with you?" he responded jauntily.

Should I let him in on all this? How will he respond? Before I could decide, Revan jumped in.

"Bill, Jane is just telling me what she's been up to. Have you heard anything about a 'mailing list issue'?"

"No. What mailing list issue?"

"Jane will tell you."

Bill surprised me. He was much more positive and supportive than Revan. Bill had taken personally Revan's defeat in the village election. Perhaps that informed his enthusiasm for my issue. In any case, while he didn't actually endorse any specific action on her part, he helped her remain sympathetic to my cause, a friend despite my less than socially acceptable behavior. I left after my tea with the impression that Revan was sympathetic if not activated.

In my indignation, and encouraged by Bill's and Revan's responses, I called several of my female friends and acquaintances in Maple Bluff, in particular the more politically powerful ones, women who were not only married to proverbial movers and shakers but who were themselves well regarded and civically active, asking them to support my effort to get the women on the mailing list. In my fervor, and despite my own hesitations and intermittent emotional struggle, I naively expected that they would embrace the cause. In each case the women acknowledged that the point was well-taken, that in fact they too believed that women "certainly ought to be included on the list like the men", but they all demurred saying such things as "I agree but I wouldn't go to the wall for this one." They all seemed nervous and agitated by the subject, just as I had been nervous and agitated when I, a supposedly liberated woman, confronted the fact that I was not being sent my government's mail—that my government might be engaged in sex discrimination.

The expression "go to the wall" expressed their sense that a simple stand for equal treatment represented extreme behavior that would precipitate extreme consequences. The image was of an execution. Perhaps for treason? Or, perhaps it was the image of women going to the wall of an embattled fortress to defend it. In any case, I heard that they weren't ready to give up everything.

Despite the fact that they foresaw dire consequences for any such effort to have all adult residents, regardless of gender, equally represented, they minimized the importance of that goal. The comment "I wouldn't go to the wall for this one" also implied the pettiness and insignificance of the issue—as though men would defend so vigorously something that had no significance. While at some level we all knew that an effort to add women to that mailing list would be punishable in the extreme, over and over again we women scoffed at the unimportance of having our names on it. "It's no big deal if our names aren't on the envelope." "I get to see the bulletin if I want to." "I don't really care whose name is on it." "You're making a mountain out of a molehill."

These moments of criticism took me back to a searing time from girlhood. I was about 9 years old. Mom was Assistant Head of my Girl Scout...or was it Brownies Troop. Gail Fallow's mother was the head of the troop and our meetings were held at her house. Gail had a beautiful bedroom complete with a white ruffled canopy bed. Everything was pink, white and ruffles. All of us girls were envious. That bedroom made Gail someone important, admired and influential amongst us. To this day I don't know how it happened but somehow something that I said about someone with no malicious intent got disseminated in our group as a nasty comment about Gail. The group turned on me. I was innocent of the charge, but felt totally impotent to prove my innocence. People talked about me behind my back and shunned me for a while. Eventually, the shunning stopped, but the wound, the trauma of being rejected by the other girls and being helpless to stop it, had remained. My fear of a repetition of this, fear that I would be rejected, ostracized, was a more powerfully paralyzing, negative force in my efforts to confront sexism, to enlist help, than I wanted to acknowledge.

When I was contemplating their resistance to my appeal for action, I saw myself through their eyes, eyes that condemned my encouragement of them to act as unnecessary trouble making. At those times my own self-doubts catalyzed by their criticism of me took control and I questioned all over again whether I was being pushy and unnecessarily needy in my demand for equal treatment.

In my moments of clarity, when I was able to self-affirm, not see myself negatively through their or my own eyes, I interpreted the negative responses of other women to my assertiveness, their questioning of whether they should make an issue of their omission from the mailing list, as simply a reflection of their own sense of low self-worth. I perceived them as self-denigrating and it saddened and frustrated me, reminding me of the classic Groucho Marx joke "I wouldn't belong to a club that would have me for a member." In these instances what I perceived as their lack of self-respect served to shock and energize me.

CHAPTER 14

While I was unsuccessfully enlisting female support, the all-male Village Board was meeting to discuss my letters, the original one intended only for the President, and the second one sent to the whole board regarding the caucus announcement. I intuited the attitude of the board by the new behavior of my male neighbors towards me. Now whenever I lunched at a local business club, a whole table of men from Maple Bluff who were regulars there simultaneously looked up from their meals to say "Hello, neighbor" as I walked by. Their behavior felt choreographed to emphasize a sarcastic use of the word "neighbor."

In January 1985 I received the Village Board's response. It arrived via a certified letter from the clerk, the paid professional administrator, not from the President or the board members, my "neighbors." As soon as I saw the officious looking envelope in the postman's hand, I knew I had been branded the enemy. Any hope that this issue would be resolved had vanished.

In response to my directive that they add my name to the official mailing list I was told that the subject was discussed at the January 1985 board meeting and action was taken at that time "to initiate the change you requested." They were putting my name on the mailing list as I instructed, but the change I "requested" to be "initiated" was the addition of *all* the women's names. To that they responded in political double speak focusing on the "manner" in which names should appear rather than the complete absence of those names: "There is no official policy regarding the manner in which village residents have their names listed on our mailing list. I will list residents' names any way they desire, all they have to do is inform me of how they want their names listed."

If "Mr. David Barry" was, to the board, simply another "manner" of saying "Mrs. David Barry," they were able to implicitly deny the exclusion of specific women's names from the list. More than once, the board members assured me that the bulletin was meant for everybody (wives as well as husbands); that when it was sent in the man's name alone to a home, that *meant* his spouse/his female house-mate as well. The man of the house being the fitting representative for his family and especially for his wife was reminiscent of the antiquated British Common Law principle of coverture whereby once married, a woman is "femme couverte." Her legal existence is subsumed under her husband. She and all her property become the property of her husband—"covered" in all senses by him. This long held phenomenon was apparently still in our collective unconscious.

Initially, I was oblivious of this implicit meaning. All I could see was that the board wasn't focusing on my concern. Any attempt to get on the list in our own right as women constituted a challenge to the existing "representative" system, where the men represented us as fathers do daughters all of our lives to the outside world.

I felt stonewalled in my attempt to correct what at least on the rational level I perceived to be a blatantly inequitable situation, which demanded change. I had approached other women for support. That hadn't worked. I had written two letters, but that had only succeeded in getting my own individual name on the list. The board had asserted that it had no policy of exclusion of women so there was no need for change. *Anyone can be on the mailing list "in any manner." All they have to do is to inform the clerk.* In essence, the village was saying that each woman had to express *individually* her desire to have her own name on the list in order to achieve representation. All the women would have to declare themselves as individual "exceptions" to the unstated, supposedly non-existent, discriminatory rule. The tacit policy of exclusion or, refusal to specifically name women, remained undisturbed.

The more I contemplated the relationship between the absence of women's names from the mailing list and our almost complete absence from the administration of our government, the more convinced I became of the integral connection between the two. *Why should we women be notified when we aren't supposed to be included in the first place, when, in fact, we are only to be represented by our men? How can we hope to achieve political parity if we aren't even notified of primary elections? Even if we are aware of the elections, if we are not specifically notified like the men, we come to the electoral process at a psychological disadvantage.* That even I entertained the idea that our absence, our exclusion, was unimportant is proof enough of my own problem. Not only were the men insensitive and unsympathetic to the issue and therefore recalcitrant to change, but so was I.

I was witness to the perspicacity of Gloria Steinem's *Revolution Within*, where she quotes a civil rights worker, E. Jack Geiger, on the damage done by racism. I saw myself in the statement:

"Of all the injuries inflicted by racism (sexism) on people of color (on women), the most corrosive is the wound within, the internalized racism (sexism) that leads some victim's at unspeakable cost to their own sense of self, to embrace the values of their oppressors." (My parentheses).

Inadvertently, I had "embraced the values of (my) oppressors." The conversion—perversion—was not so total that I rejected the ideal of equality. I still consciously agreed in principle that "women ought to be treated as equals," but often when the time had come to implement this belief by actively opposing subordination, I had either rejected the notion that each incident was an instance of a general pattern, managed to see the instance as so minor, so petty, it was unworthy of my opposition, personally avoided its effects by invoking and hiding behind my perceived identity as an exception to the rule of male primacy, or found it an epic battle to face reality.

I had internalized sexism. It was my own subconscious view that women were ordained inferior and thus deserving of subordination to men, in short, my sociologically inculcated lack of self-esteem, that caused me to perceive the inequities suffered by us as "minor," and "unimportant." This same internalized sexism caused me to conceive of any woman who opposed discrimination as unnecessarily disruptive, petty, neurotically self-centered and ultimately damned by God as well as by man. Because I subconsciously embraced sexist values, I had lived a bifurcated existence, clinging to the illusion of my own equality with men—there is no problem—while actually living life as a token and therefore as an inferior.

But this time there was no place to hide. Before the mailing list issue I could ignore instances of subordination because I was able to convince myself that at least I, personally, had either avoided or negotiated my own exemption from such treatment. This time when the token (the inclusion of my name on the mailing list) making me an exception, was offered, I had to confront the fact that it was meaningless. This time it was clear that the insult of exclusion which continued to be perpetrated against my fellow female citizens *was actually being perpetrated on me as well,* whether they included me on the mailing list or not. In a democracy where the majority rules, my interests as a woman could not be equally served if all women were not equally included. As a woman, my identity as just another second-class citizen in Maple Bluff could no longer be denied. I could no longer deceive myself that I was any different from all the other subordinated women. I, too, was excluded from true parity.

Until now I had seen the male supremacy of sexism as benign. Declaring myself unaffected, exempt as an exception to female inferiority and its deserved subordination, I had implicitly and inadvertently, endorsed it. Sexism had been there all the time, but I had chosen not to acknowledge or act against it. I had self-deluded convincing myself that despite the fact that I am a woman I was not like other women. I had subconsciously used the idea of being an exception as a way to prove to myself that I was not inferior or subordinate, to escape confronting my own feelings of inadequacy, when that's exactly what, and how, I felt. I had settled for the illusion of equality in a sexist society.

Women's interests had finally become my interest. Reluctantly, the cheerleader had become an active feminist.

*

Although the 3rd of April 1985 was an innocuous enough, early, spring day in Madison, WI with the temperature a relatively benign mid 50's, no meteorological threats, I embarked on the threatening and treacherous 3.5-mile journey to the Equal Rights Division of the Wisconsin Department of Industry, Labor and Human Relations in downtown Madison. At the advice of a lawyer friend I had completed a form charging the Maple Bluff Village Board with sex discrimination.

The office was huge, institutional, impersonal with florescent lights, nondescript, beige walls adorned with black and white signs, a disinterested secretary sitting at a gray metal desk, the din from bureaucrats on telephones presumably talking to other people about other complaints. I had made an appointment, so when the secretary signaled she was ready for me, I gave my name—quietly. I wanted help, but I hoped no one I knew was there to witness my presence. In what sounded to me like a magnified public address system response, she said: "Ok, MRS. BARRY, take a seat. I'll let the lawyer know you are here."

I thought: *Did anyone hear my name? God, please modulate your voice, lady!* I just wanted to file my complaint *quietly*, have the State Board look into it and, hopefully, tell the village that they should desist from discriminating against their female constituents.

After a few agonizing minutes in the waiting room, a gray-haired man opened his office door and called out: "Is there a JANE BARRY HERE?"

I swear...is he using a loudspeaker?

I jumped up, grabbed the file folder I'd brought and scurried into the protective privacy of his office. He returned to his seat and without so much as glancing at me, said "Have a seat" signaling with the flick of his hand for me to take the chair in front of his desk.

Looking down at his desk, preoccupied, moving some papers around, he said in a voice without affect: "So, Mrs. Barry, what brings you here today?" His tone evinced the same level of interest my doctor's does when I tell him something like I need my ears irrigated.

"I'm hoping that you can help me get the Maple Bluff Village Board to make their mailing list non-discriminatory."

He stopped moving the items on his desk and looked up at me for the first time. Then, he looked down at his desk and picked up: "Summary of complaint." He obviously hadn't had a chance to read it before this moment because only now was his interest piqued. Maple Bluff is a power center, not only in Madison but also in the state. It is the perennial residence of every Governor of the State of Wisconsin because the Governor's Mansion is situated in the village. The State's Attorney General, the owner of Rayovac, the real Oscar Mayer of hotdog fame and many other powerbrokers lived there.

Then he looked me directly in the eye: "Tell me more about this."

I opened my file folder containing my copy of the Complaint, village bulletins announcing caucus meetings addressed only to Dave, a copy of the all-male mailing list, the letters I had written, a copy of the real estate tax bill with both our names on it and finally, the board's certified response to my second letter admitting nothing and making no meaningful changes, except the sole addition of my name. Encouraged by him to dilate on the issue, I told him the whole story. I implored him to keep the thing under wraps, informing him that I hoped to accomplish change with as little collateral damage to my business, my social life and to the village's public image as possible.

He said: "Look, Mrs. Barry, I won't say anything to the press, but there are no guarantees this will not be publicized since the local reporters monitor the proceedings of the ERD. They have a right to do so and they will certainly take an interest in this filing."

Disappointed by this information, I, reluctantly, accepted; although the Equal Rights Division had no authority to coerce compliance with its judgment, I was hoping that if they decided that "probable cause" existed to believe that the village was acting illegally, my position would gain credibility. I hoped a favorable decision would cause the board members to change their ways in order to avoid the threat of more negative publicity. The ERD complaint seemed more prudent, politically, socially and financially, than launching a lawsuit. In point of fact, I simply didn't have enough confidence that I was "right" to file suit. I needed the validation of the Equal Rights Division. I wanted, needed, someone in authority *with* me, someone or something to agree with me and be an intermediary between me and the powers that be.

*

In June I found a letter from the Equal Rights Division in our mailbox; I ran into the house waving the letter: "Dave!...Dave! Where are you?"

"Here, in the family room! What's up?"

I burst in, my hands shaking: "It's here! The ERD decision is here!" I held the unopened envelope up to him.

"Well, don't just stand there! Open it! What does it say?"

Heart in my mouth, I opened the letter and began to read:

"There is probable cause to believe that the Respondent (Village of Maple Bluff) discriminated against the Complainant because of sex in regard to the providing of services in violation of Wisconsin Statues 942,04..."

"Whoohoo! Yeah! It's over! Thank goodness! Now, the board *will have to act* to change things. It's no longer just me telling them. It's the

139

state for God's sake! They won't want to go against the STATE! What a relief to know that they can't just dismiss me as some crazy kook."

Dave was happy that the ruling was in my favor but he was more cynical than I, a lot less sanguine that this was the end of it. He tried to let me down gently: "Jane, you've got good reason to be happy that the Equal Rights Division has ruled in your favor. It does give you credibility, but this ruling probably won't stop them. The board is likely to resist despite this ruling."

"You think so? NO! I don't think they would defy the State.

Well, Dave, in any case, I'm sure that there will be a board meeting about this ruling and I will go to it to make sure that it's implemented."

I was much more optimistic than Dave. I could not conceive that given a ruling by the State, that the village board would violate it.

The night the ERD decision was on the agenda at the board meeting, two of my immediate neighbors who were interested in the issue attended the meeting with me. The only other attendees were the board members themselves. There were 5 of them. When I entered the boardroom, they were all seated at the front at a table on a dais wearing business suits and engaged in conversation amongst themselves. I knew two of them well from parties Dave and I attended in better days. When the time came for consideration of the ERD judgment, one of the board members, a man of about 60, ruddy faced, overweight and a member of one of the old-line families in the village, turned to me:

"Mrs. Barry, would you be so kind as to answer some questions for this board?"

Immediately, I sensed hostility. First, he didn't smile or try in any way to ingratiate himself with me and his verbal expression "would you be so kind," had a distinct edge to it as though he was almost insinuating that he fully expected that I was not "kindly." The 'coup de grace' was that this man had always called me familiarly "Jane." For him to address me as Mrs. Barry felt denigrating, as if he refused to grant me my given name, wanting to subordinate me under my husband. Whether or not he was attempting to put me in my place as a wife who in his mind should not be causing trouble, but instead should act like the biblical, "virtuous woman," he was definitely distancing himself from me by his very formality.

I responded: "Why yes, of course, John." I was trying to reinstate our social relationship.

He was having none of it: "First, how do you want to be addressed? Shall I call you 'Jane,' 'Mrs. Barry,' or perhaps 'Ms. Barry'?

"It doesn't matter. Whichever you'd like."

"Well, Mrs. Barry," (*for sure, he will not be enticed to be social*) "how do *you* want *us* to designate all the other women on the mailing list: Ms., Miss, Mrs. or do *you* want us to use their first and last names?"

I see where this is going. He's directing the conversation to the issue of "manner" of address and away from the relevant issue of the absolute absence of the women from the mailing list.

"I am not here to make those decisions, John. I am simply asking that you include the women of this village on our mailing list. How you designate them is up to you and them, I suppose."

Another man, unknown to me, chimed in:

"Well, Mrs. Barry, what are we to do in instances in which women do not want their names on the list?"

Before I could answer another man asked:

"Oh, and do you want us to send out *two* envelopes to every home, one to the man and one to the woman or would you be satisfied if we put both names on one envelope?"

I get it. The implication of most of these questions is that I am a 'prima donna,' a troublemaker, an agitator, demanding and presumptuous to boot; the issue of the mailing list frivolous, unimportant, petty and a royal pain in the ass.

One of the board members I did know, who had always been pleasant to me, but significantly, a man who owned multiple cars, each one of them bearing his initials alone but a numeral designating the member of the family who drove it, number 1 for him, number two being his wife, and so on hierarchically down through his kids, suddenly erupted. Sweat dripping from his forehead, he pointed menacingly at me and all but yelled:

"Jane, I just want you to know that I think you are a BAD NEIGHBOR for going to the Wisconsin Equal Rights Division with this complaint!"

I thought he was going to call me a BITCH or some other swear word, so his words were almost comically mild, but I was taken aback by the vituperation with which they were expressed.

Before I could respond, my next-door neighbor, an intelligent, enlightened woman who had been divorced for many years, lived alone, but as a mother of five grown children, had always embraced our children and me and Dave, mounted a spirited defense of my neighborliness:

"Jim, I want to say that I object to your calling Jane a 'bad neighbor.' I live right next door to her. I know her very well and I can vouch for the fact that she is a very good neighbor!"

I was surprised and grateful for her enthusiastic endorsement but ultimately it did little to impact the results. The Chairman of the Board put an end to this exchange:

"Mrs. Barry, if you don't like the way we run things here in Maple Bluff, you might just want to move out of the village because we have no intention of changing our mailing list for you."

God! Dave was right. The ERD's decision involved no penalty, basically had no teeth. So it meant that they would resist. I was hoping for acquiescence but I had heeded Dave's warning. I was ready. I stood, gathered my belongings as if to leave, but stopped and turned to the board:

"I regret your decision, but in view of it, I have a short statement that I would like to read:

142

'On June 4, 1985 the State of Wisconsin Department of Industry Labor and Human Relations Equal Rights Division stated: 'There is probable cause to believe that the Maple Bluff Village Board of Trustees discriminated against Jane Barry because of sex.' Whether this discrimination violates Statute 942, Statute 347 or Statute XYZ is immaterial! What is relevant is that I and all the other women excluded from receipt of official bulletins are being discriminated against. I am tired of the board's resorting to legal technicalities instead of addressing the discrimination substantially and I want you to know that I intend to see that the discrimination is terminated. If you force me to resort to legal measures, which will be much costlier to our village both financially and politically, I will do so, but the responsibility will be on your heads. I urge you to consider your action carefully."

"Mrs. Barry, we will not be threatened by you."

"I am not threatening anyone. I am simply informing you that I don't intend to let the matter die."

"Good night, Mrs. Barry," and with that I was peremptorily dismissed.

On the way home from that meeting, I was agitated. If I held my position, the only course of action left me was to file a lawsuit against the village. I couldn't envision doing that! My legal experiences had been confined to routine real estate business transactions. The thought of actually suing somebody, much less my government, was not only daunting but also felt presumptuous—even outrageous.

Nevertheless, the alternative, to simply drop the matter, to ignore the humiliating fact that we women were being held equally liable for the taxes but not provided the same services, would be unacceptable.

Still there was the issue of the social, professional and financial costs of continuing. I was irritated by the patronizing treatment but did I want to put my whole lifestyle in jeopardy by doing something so controversial? While I was ignorant of the actual dynamics of retribution and the extent to which the enemies I was making might adversely affect my life, I was aware that there probably would be an effect.

Dave was still up, waiting in the family room for me. I told him what had transpired.

"Well, Jane, you know that I'm not surprised. I told you patriarchs don't like a woman telling them what to do! They think you're just causing trouble. So, what are you going to do now?"

There was my typical Dave, again. He never wanted to discuss an issue unless there was some action to be taken to deal with it, but I hadn't come to a decision: "Oh, God, I don't know! I mean it's degrading to know that you are being discriminated against and then not to do anything to stop it, but I know that if I go any further with this, my only alternative is a lawsuit! What will that do to our social life? What will that do to my business? Can we afford it? I mean it's a big decision that impacts our whole family."

Dave got up from his chair, stretched, and said: "Well, I'm going to bed." Then he turned, looked me directly in the eye and smiled: "Honey, let me know what you decide. Either way, I'm on your side. Night." And off he went leaving me with my issue.

Dave as always had given me room to think, to come to my own conclusions. I appreciate that about him. In that moment, I knew that he meant well; that he was not leaving me out of lack of interest or concern, but rather respect. Still, there was certainly a part of me that would have just liked him to give me the solution. *Tell me what to do!*

I paced around the house until the early morning hours, too keyed up to sleep. At about 2:30 A.M. on my way to bed I happened by the big mirror in the front hall wherein I caught a glimpse of my reflection. As I studied it, appalled at how tired, haggard, wrinkled and unattractive I looked, it occurred to me that despite my concerns about public opinion, my worries that if I pursued the issue of the sexist mailing list, many conventional types would criticize me to the point of our social life and my business suffering, what mattered ultimately *was my own* opinion of myself: *How will I feel about myself 20, 40 years from now if I back away from such an important ideal as equality just because I don't want to incur the wrath of these 5 or 6 paunchy, middle-aged reactionaries on the Village Board? If I live to be an old woman, most of them, being about 10 to 20 years older than I, will be dead already and I will have forsaken a principle I consider sacred simply to court popularity with them. My face then will surely be ugly to me, not only marred by the normal lines and sags of age, but it'll be the face of a coward, of a woman who has sold out.*

*

On July 3, 1985, a month after the board meeting, I filed suit against the Village of Maple Bluff alleging violation of my civil rights as a woman denied access to the government equal to that enjoyed by the men.

CHAPTER 15

Filing suit against the Village of Maple Bluff led to a dramatic change in our family's life. Every social outing became a journey into the unknown.

*

Dave and I were attending a neighborhood fund-raiser for a liberal candidate for judge. There, we met some of our more socially prominent "friends", a couple who owned one of the most impressive homes in Maple Bluff and in the Madison area, a well-known stop on the social circuit. In the days before the lawsuit, we had been frequent guests there. Born and raised in Wisconsin, the son of an influential family, he was definitely one of the "good ol' boys". He had friends in high places, lots of political clout and was himself a portly patriarch. She seemed to me a liberated, career woman.

As she approached me, I smiled, assuming that she was just being sociable. She was a chic dresser with streaked hair, the requisite tan from the requisite trip south to avoid the harsh Wisconsin winter and a neat well-honed figure.

"Jane, I hear you filed a lawsuit against the village."

She had evidently seen the article in the Wisconsin State Journal newspaper. She paused and just as I was about to respond, cut me off with: "That's going a bit far...don't you think? You are causing unnecessary trouble for the village."

Until that night I was an idealist. I'd have bet that she would have been on my side in the mailing list issue, that she would have agreed that it was only right that the female citizens be notified of caucuses and all other legal and significant issues affecting the village. I believed her "liberated" facade—as I believed my own—but tonight I learned differently.

Months later, there was the big Christmas party at the home of a scion of Maple Bluff society, the heir to a successful regional manufacturing company. The house was on one of the most spectacular lots in "the Bluff" sitting high overlooking Lake Mendota with an unobstructed view of the impressive state capitol building. The owner liked Dave, and I played in a tennis group with his wife, so despite my recent activism, we were included in their huge Christmas open house. Everyone who was anyone was there. Since invitations were becoming less frequent, this one was appreciated. I made a real effort to dress nicely for the occasion.

Entering their large dining room, I saw it festooned with luxurious Christmas decorations and the table laden with rich offerings: a whole smoked salmon decorated with cucumber rings garnished with capers, lemons and parsley; delicate, puff pastries with a variety of tasty fillings; tiny lamb chops and a tempting assortment of desserts. The crush around the table, the high-spirited chatter of people in the holiday mood all helped me forget that I was not the social butterfly I once was. Then suddenly, a man whose wife had attended Smith College—but hadn't graduated—turned to me and asked if I still volunteered for Smith. I had been a volunteer alumnae contact for local girls who were applicants to the college; I helped with capital campaigns for the college and ran the Madison area Smith College alumnae group for years. I was complimented to think that Josh knew about my Smith involvement. When I answered in the affirmative, he unexpectedly scowled, his face becoming red with repressed emotion. He virtually spit out the next words:

"Well, my wife certainly wouldn't participate in Smith activities. She disapproves of the feminist thrust at Smith. She's a 'real woman'—not a man-hating lesbian."

Ironically as he delivered his message, I received it, looking like the epitome of a 'real woman,' dressed as I was in one of my most glamorous outfits: a long, slinky, knitted black dress with a strand of opera length pearls and a 1930's grey fox boa I had found at an estate sale that very afternoon. I looked as much the movie star as I ever have and probably ever will.

Since I recognized he was inebriated in the extreme, I decided not to argue but rather to minimize the encounter simply saying: "I understand you feel that way, Josh."

*

At another cocktail party, I was standing beside a man at a buffet table. When I reached for something diagonally in front of me, but directly in front of my neighbor at the table, I suddenly realized I might be irritating him so I quickly withdrew my hand only to hear him declare in stentorian tones, audible to all in the vicinity:

"Jane, EXCUSE YOU, but what more would one expect from Jane Barry? Why she's the rudest woman I know."

Before my activism my relationship with him and the other fellows was always cordial. After, I was a man-hating lesbian and "rude and pushy."

*

But it wasn't until I was snubbed at a funeral that I knew the extent of the ostracism I was facing. Dave and I were attending a post funeral gathering given by the bereaved family in the basement of the local Episcopal Church. Funeral gatherings had become one of our only social outlets. One didn't need an invitation. Everyone in the neighborhood was there. About ten minutes after we arrived, I found myself in the middle of the room, squashed among the throng and face-to-face with the husband of a woman with whom I had had a longstanding casual friendship. Our kids always frolicked at the same club pool every summer.

The husband had a long lineage in the Village of Maple Bluff. His family owned a local lumber company. A tall, lanky, rather attractive looking man in his early forties, Kevin was the son of privilege. He grew up in one of the grander homes on the lake, learned to play tennis and golf at an early age at the neighborhood country club and always dressed the part of the country club set. He always appeared to me to be very conventional and the relationship between him and his wife reminiscent of the Cleaver's, but despite a naturally subdued manner he had always been cordial to me.

When I recognized him, I addressed him familiarly by name: "Hi, Kevin. How are you?" I said expecting a friendly response.

The words were barely out of my mouth when he gave me a cold, hard stare and then did an abrupt quarter-turn in place leaving me staring at his shoulder. I experienced first-hand the probable sociological origin of the phrase "the cold shoulder." When you couldn't bond at a funeral where everyone forgives everyone's peccadilloes in the context of a keen appreciation for the shared brevity of life, you know you're in deep trouble socially.

*

The most distressing fallout from my activism was the difficulty our eldest daughter, Neville, experienced. At the time she was 10 years old. Her playmates were the sons and daughters of influential Maple Bluff people who were now rejecting me and my stand. Their kids were beginning to haze her. This shocked me. I couldn't believe that the parents would allow their sons and daughters to turn against innocent Neville on account of my political action but that was the case. She was no longer invited to their homes for anything.

It got so bad that Dave and I decided to look for a house on the other side of Madison, outside Maple Bluff. We wanted to get Neville out of the line of fire.

Not far into our search for a new homestead, we found one that we wanted her to see. When we told her about it, we were surprised by her response. She listened to our description: "Neville, I think that you will like it. It's in Shorewood Hills, near your friend's house. It's a two story, just like this one, but it's wood, not brick. It has 4 bedrooms just like this one and has a nice lot. We'd like to show it to you tomorrow."

Then she quietly said: "Mom, Dad, I know you are trying to make things easier for me. I don't like what's been happening either, that the kids are turning against me, too..." and there was a pause while the expression on her face turned from contemplative to combative, "but I am not going to be forced out of my own neighborhood by these kids! I've got other friends at my school. I'll spend more time with them. The heck with these kids who are being mean!"

Dave and I were impressed. "Ok, Neville, if you think you can handle this, we won't move. Just let us know if it gets too hard."

Although I would never want to see any of my children endure that again, Neville was emerging from her painful experience stronger than I was at her age. She had already experienced rejection by her peers and survived, a good, though painful, lesson.

*

If my challenge to the male power structure of the village had caused a disruption in our social life, my challenge to my father's supremacy had produced a similar response in my family life. When he and my mother were leaving to drive back home after a Thanksgiving visit, a scene occurred between me and my dad in the front hall of our house. Mom was already out at the car with our kids and Dave was there with them. I was on my way out the door to say goodbye. Dad came back in to catch me before I emerged:

"Jane, I just want you to know that your mother and I will not be coming out here again to see you and Dave." I was thunderstruck trying to compute what he just said. *He's not ever coming here again to see us?*

Before I could recover and respond, he clarified: "We will only come here to see the grandkids. We love them very much and do still want to see them."

"What?" I said, not quite understanding.

"You heard me. We will come here again, but not to see you and Dave, just to see the kids...we don't like the way you have treated us."

I was totally confounded. I didn't know what to say except to resort to my the script from the therapist: "I'm sad you feel that way Dad. I sure didn't mean to mistreat you."

He didn't raise his voice at all. Just very quietly he said: "Well, you did. So, that's the way it will be." And then he left me in the hall without a kiss or a hug. I was so stunned, I just stood there, reeling. The next thing I knew the kids burst through the front door, somewhat bewildered yelling "Mom, why didn't you come out? You missed them! Grandpa and Grandma are gone!"

Gone. Mom and Dad were gone.

Another cold—much colder—shoulder. Dad didn't explicitly disavow his familial relationship to me; however, by telling me that he was no longer coming to see me, but only my children, he was, implicitly, cutting it off.

There was the "monastery incident" from which I can only assume he never had recovered, but there had been other incidents, too—all of which reinforced the idea that my priority was my role as a wife, mother and businesswoman as opposed to an eternal daughter. Although Dad didn't elaborate on the specific impetus for this statement, I think that it was precipitated by something that had occurred on that particular Thanksgiving visit.

He and Mom told me that they would be arriving sometime on the

Tuesday before Thanksgiving, most likely around dinnertime. They were driving from Boston to Madison and stopping overnight at friends' along the way so their ETA could not be exact. I said that was fine, but I emphasized that, should they arrive earlier than dinnertime, they should come to my office in downtown Madison rather than to the house. In fact, they did arrive early but instead of following my instructions, they went directly to the house because it was lunchtime. Dave was there with Lydia, 3, and Margaret 1. He had picked Lydia up from pre-school and just finished giving both their lunch when my parents knocked on the door. He was totally unprepared to host them, expecting they would have gone to my office if they arrived before dinner. He asked them to follow the plan. They were irate with Dave's dismissal. When they complained to me, I defended Dave, telling them that he was probably harassed by the two kids, not expecting them and therefore unprepared. That didn't mollify them. They were hurt. I felt bad, but Dave and I had worked out a schedule and I had let them know.

I never had many conversations with Dad, but I had always felt loved and appreciated by him. This announcement that he and my mother would no longer come to see me, only my kids, was a shock to my system, not because things would change that much day to day, but to know that Dad didn't want anything to do with me except as a grandfather to my children was shocking and very painful. A real adjustment.

All forms of patrimony ceased. Knowledgeable and talented in all aspects of electronics, mechanics and plumbing, Dad had always helped us with any repairs whenever he has visited. No more. He never announced his resignation. Instead, he no longer brought his toolbox on visits. In fact, if any kind of household problems arose in his presence, he'd sit inert, an act which for my father must have required supreme effort. Such behavior ran counter to his nature as a 'doer'.

At Christmas my parents had always been generous, sending a big box of presents. After the Thanksgiving incident the same sized box still arrived but with almost nothing for Dave and me. Everything was for the grandchildren.

I didn't consciously anticipate the ultimate extent of the consequences for persisting in my demand for equal adulthood. In the case of my father, I knew that if I resisted his desire to stay at our house, he would be angry, yes, but he would get over his anger. *After all, he is my Dad.* His love for me would temper his irritation. Inadvertently, I seemed to have perpetrated a kind of unforgivable treachery that couldn't be overlooked: violation of his primacy? He now withheld his fatherly affections and tokens. I was in effect disowned.

*

There's a graphic German word that describes what I did when I took action against female subordination in Maple Bluff and in my family. That word is 'nestbesmirchen.' It means exactly as it sounds: I had 'besmirched my own nest'. My social, professional and personal lives were a mess. For someone who had always been socially and economically ambitious, I was—as my husband was wont to remark—by dint of hard work "clawing my way to the bottom." For a daughter who was the 'apple of her father's eye', I had certainly lost that status.

I struggled with my new identity as an activist and alien. One minute I was filled with conviction that the chosen course was right; that I should, therefore, forge valiantly ahead working for change. The next minute I was filled with despair and sadness that I was not achieving in the traditional way anymore and that even my relationship with my parents had become strained, if not totally destroyed.

I had lived by a ditty taught to me years before by my mother in her role as my Assistant Girl Scout Leader: "Make new friends and keep the old. One is silver and the other gold." Now I didn't seem to be making many new friends or keeping the old, evidently one of the prices of taking my place as an equal adult in my world.

When I walked in my neighborhood, people who were outside their homes regularly disappeared inside or pretended preoccupation to avoid me. If I bumped into an acquaintance in the supermarket, someone who in the past would have stopped to chat, any exchange was now short-lived. In fact, I practically had to bump into them, literally, to have any conversation at all. Otherwise, my former friends were like leaves before a blower, I being the blower.

One of my few remaining friends, Revan, told me that she overheard this exchange at one of the many parties to which Dave and I weren't invited. When someone mentioned my name, another guest who was trying to determine if she knew me, asked: "Jane Barry? Now she's that Communist, isn't she?"

My friend interjected: "Not exactly. She's a real estate broker!"

Little did anyone know, but many nights I woke up at 3 AM, the proverbial 'hour of the wolf, in the total dark when there wasn't a sound in the house' tormented, feeling alone, frightened, asking myself why I had taken such a drastic step. I was totally certain that I was perverse for suing my government. I was pained that people didn't like me anymore; that my business was suffering; that my children were being excluded from parties they would normally be invited to and that our funds were being depleted by the cost of the lawsuit. I was enduring a nauseating rollercoaster of emotions.

During most daylight hours my rational side prevailed and I understood the importance of my lawsuit. Dave was there and we often remarked on the significance of what may have seemed like a trivial situation, the lack of women's names on a mailing list. We realized, though, that by fighting the "little" thing, I was challenging the big thing; that once you allow the little things to occur, the big things follow; that the little things are symbolic, microcosmic manifestations of the big. But at night, fear and self-doubt overwhelmed me. When Dave would be awakened by the change in the cadence of my breathing and sometimes by my sobbing, he'd exhort me, assuring me that I was doing the right thing. *Thank God for him. He is helping me to endure.*

It took almost two years, close to $10,000 of our money for legal fees, and much emotional discomfort, but I prevailed in the lawsuit. The judge ordered the village to reimburse all my legal fees and make the mailing list non-discriminatory. The law professor husband of a fellow Smith alum in Madison later told me that the issue of the mailing list, since it involved electoral access, was a constitutional issue.

The village board did the least possible, addressing the village bulletin to "Resident" rather than simply adding the females' names, all of which I had provided to them, to the extant list, but the principle prevailed. Men and women were now technically treated as equals with regard to the dissemination of public notices in the village of Maple Bluff. I was proud of that. In addition, during and right after my suit there was a succession of female members on the Village Board, one even serving as its President. And, the village hired a female, professional administrator as well. She was the only woman to serve in that position with the exception being during WWII when there were no men available. She proved to be a consummate professional.

I was gratified that these changes occurred but I would be lying if I didn't admit that I felt anger that the Village Board made the list impersonal, especially after I did all the work to give them a complete list of the village's female residents. It felt like a petty rebuke of me for forcing them to change their ways. Even if we were not honored by being explicitly and specifically included, I needed and wanted to accept the good, the fact that women were no longer discriminated against on the mailing list. Women serving on the board and as Village Administrator was a direct result of my lawsuit, which highlighted the exclusion of women and prompted the public, maybe even the women, to become conscious of our absence from the government of the village. Despite my conviction that my actions led to this positive result, I did feel frustrated that while other women were benefitting, I was not, nor did I get any credit. I'm not such a selfless person that I wouldn't have enjoyed some praise. So, I did the only thing I could: I gave myself the ticket. I respected myself for what I did.

CHAPTER 16

In a sense, having become a pariah in my neighborhood and being disapproved of by my parents freed me. I had little else to lose. Unpopularity had always been a threatening prospect for me, but I was becoming acclimated to it. The world hadn't fallen off its axis; I hadn't died just because I was disapproved. I no longer was succumbing to the temptation to avoid challenging unequal treatment. I no longer minimized, rationalized or ignored the problem. I saw it for what it was; I trusted my perception and I confronted issues head on.

*

For our twentieth wedding anniversary in August of '88 I engaged a room at a posh, private, men's business club in Chicago where I had reciprocal privileges through my membership in the Madison Club, the local business club. When I called the Chicago club to reserve the room, the clerk asked for my husband's name and membership number. I gave him Dave's name but emphasized that *I* was the member of the Madison Club, not my husband.

When we arrived for our stay I registered, at which point the receptionist asked me for my husband's membership number. Again, I clarified that *I* was the member and again provided my Madison Club membership number.

When we finished our anniversary dinner in the club dining room, a part of my anniversary gift to Dave, the waiter automatically placed the check at Dave's plate. Immediately reacting, Dave said:

"Excuse me, Sir, but I am the guest, *my wife* here is the member and she should get the bill."

Irritated, the waiter rolled his eyes, smirked slightly and shoved the bill my way, but not without a snide: "Madam, you *do* have a guest membership card, I presume?"

"Oh, yes, of course," I replied.

With that I proudly reached into my purse. As I prepared to hand it over, I noticed that it said: *This is to certify that David S. Barry is a Guest Member.*

Chagrined, I looked up to meet his hostile gaze: "I thought I had a membership card, but it seems I don't."

I turned to Dave, incredulous: "This card has been issued in your name!"

Beckoning to the maître d', I held the card up and pointed at the name: "There seems to be an error. My guest member card has been issued in my husband's name. He is not the member of the affiliate club. Would you please have this corrected for me so I can take care of the dinner charges?"

"Oh, it doesn't matter, Madam. You can still use it," he said, his tone betraying some annoyance with my perceived perfectionism.

A moment earlier when my husband had informed the waiter that he was my guest, the waiter had demanded that I produce my membership card. Now, my objection to the erroneous card is an unnecessary bother to the maître d'! He dismisses the mistake as inconsequential.

"No," I persisted. "I don't want to use this card because it is not mine. I'd like to have my own card."

"Ma'am, it's not necessary. I'll simply use this card," he said reaching to wrest it from me.

I pulled the card back. "No...I would like a correct card. I don't want to use this one. It's not mine to use!" I practically shouted, avoiding his grasp.

Now, we were both good and miffed.

"Well, *do* what you want," he virtually spit as he disdainfully exaggerated the enunciation of the dental consonants, his "d's" and "t's," hesitating ominously between each word, "But *I* need a card to charge this meal to."

With that, I begrudgingly handed him the defective card. He wrote down the member number and both waiter and maître d' departed.

My head was pounding and I felt vaguely nauseated. Our delicious meal was ruined. I was upset and angry at not being accorded the respect to which my membership entitled me; yet, I was also struggling with feelings of discomfort because of the obvious opinion of the club staff that I was being a bitch for wanting to be acknowledged and treated as a legitimate club member.

On the way back to our room, I fulminated about the incident:

"Did you hear that guy, Dave?! First, he grills me about having a membership card, implying I'm not authorized to have you as my guest. Then, when I realize that I don't even have a membership card because they've issued me a membership in *your* name when you have absolutely *NO* relationship to this Club or to the Madison Club, he trivializes their error. Can you believe it? Both he and the maître d' were actually exasperated that *I* should want the card in my own name!—like I'm some sort of a pain in the ass bitch because I want a correct card reflecting my affiliate membership, the perks of the membership fees I pay."

Dave had little patience with complaining and, as usual, was more focused on action: "Well, Jane, what are you going to *do*? Are you just going to let it go—or do you want to *do* something about it? You gave the maître d' the card with my name on it. Is that the end of it? He's happy. It's over for him." He stopped talking.

I was still mulling over his question when he spoke again.

"I don't know what *you're* going to do, Jane, but I know what I'm going to do. I'm going to write a letter to the manager of this place letting him know that I don't appreciate the automatic assumption that I am responsible for every bill—even when I am the guest!"

Facing forward, his head held high, only the dimple in his cheek and the sparkle in the corner of his eye betrayed the mischief he was brewing.

If he had remained silent or simply offered some sympathetic comment like "Yeah, it's terrible that you were treated that way," my indignation may have dissipated without any counter attack, but I knew the dinner would not have been redeemed. It would have remained a miserable memory.

Instead Dave had pointed the way toward a dignified response. "Good idea, I said. We'll *both* write the manager: you about being presented with bills and obligations at every turn when you are, in fact, an invited guest; I about not being treated like the member I am. In fact, if you will give me your letter, I will leave our two letters in lieu of payment of my bill!"

They're not simply dealing with "a bitch"; this bitch has an ally, a male ally.

The bill for our stay was over $300. As we departed, I went to the front desk and delivered the two letters addressed to the Manager. Then I walked out the door.

Several weeks later I received my monthly statement from my own club in Madison. It contained the charges incurred at the Chicago affiliate. I called the Madison Club Manager explaining the situation and awaited my club's response. Soon I received a censure from my club's board for my "failure to pay charges incurred" in my Chicago stay and a repeat of the bill. To convince the board to reconsider its position I decided to allow them to experience the same kind of indignity perpetrated by the Chicago affiliate on me and Dave. I drafted a letter detailing my entire experience, but instead of addressing that letter to the actual board members of my home club (all of whom were male), I addressed my letter to their wives, implicitly defining *the wives* as the Directors of the club. Just as my membership had been unilaterally stripped from me and bestowed on my spouse, so I stripped their Directorships from them and

162

conferred them on their wives.

At the last minute I decided not to send the letters to the spouses, realizing that while such a ploy satisfied my desire for vengeance, it was inconsiderate to innocent bystanders, their wives. Instead I sent the letters I had written for their wives along with a cover letter to each of the board members suggesting that they consider how they would feel had I persisted in my original plan to ignore them and involve their spouses. I appealed to their empathy.

At their next meeting they voted to pay the charge I had incurred at the sexist club.

Further, at my suggestion, a letter was sent to all our club's affiliates throughout the world asserting that our club expected all of its members, male and female, to be treated equally and with dignity at affiliate clubs; that in the event such is not the case, our club would not honor any obligation to make restitution for any unpaid bills incumbent on discriminatory treatment.

I was becoming accustomed to claiming my equal adulthood.

CHAPTER 17

My demand for equal adulthood had led inevitably to another epiphany in 1989. For over a decade since 1974 I had considered myself a member of The Maple Bluff Country Club, the country club that rented and occupied one third of the public land in our village. Yes, I had been aware that I was not allowed in the male-only Grille Room without a male companion—and then only one night a week; that the club had more limited (and segregated) hours for women on the golf course and driving range, and that there were reportedly gross inequities in amenities in the male and female locker rooms facilities and services, but, somehow, amazingly, it had never occurred to me that these disparities might have been an indication of an unequal status of men and women in the club. Further, I had reasoned that if I didn't like things, I didn't have to belong to the country club.

Well, the joke was on me. I actually didn't belong to the club! I hadn't been an unequal member...I was not a member at all! Just "the spouse of a member."

Again, I was shocked and frankly embarrassed at my own prolonged stupidity. I had been participating in the club for over a decade, volunteering for tasks, taking my children there, attending the club parties, playing tennis, swimming in the pool, paying the monthly bill and considering myself a member but I didn't even belong! Dave did, not I.

That evening back in 1973 when Dave and I attended the club's "New Members' Reception" suddenly made complete sense:

As we had approached the greeter in the foyer, a balding man in his sixties who was a Vice-President of a large national corporation and a Board Member of the Club, he was cordial, but he seemed nervous.

Standing by a table with typed nametags on it, he asked our names and then selected an elegantly raised printed one that said: *David S. Barry, III*

Looking again at the table and then at me, he said sheepishly:

"I'm sorry, Mrs. Barry, but I can't seem to find your name tag here. Please wait. I'll be right back." And off he scurried, muttering and obviously flustered.

Neither Dave nor I got the picture. We just waited, oblivious to the chaos we must have been creating behind the scenes as they tried to find a spare name tag and magic marker to create one for me. A few minutes later the man appeared breathless:

"Here, Mrs. Barry," he said as he handed me a crude, handcrafted facsimile, Mrs. David S. Barry III nametag: "I apologize for this makeshift nametag."

I thanked him for his efforts, pinned it on my dress and proceeded into the dining room with Dave where I immediately spotted Tim, another one of the club's board members, a man we knew as "our sponsor."

We were introduced to Tim several months earlier at a cocktail party given by a mutual friend, Bronson La Follette, erstwhile Attorney General of the state of Wisconsin, for the express purpose of providing us with a club sponsor. At that party I had my first (and last) scotch and soda. Oysters, a favorite of mine, were also served. About a half hour into the party, I felt suddenly, violently nauseous. Unfortunately, at that moment I was engaged in conversation with our prospective sponsor. In mid-sentence I tried to swallow hard, but instead, projectile vomited right at him. Luckily, the missile fell slightly short so I missed him, but I made quite an impression on the poor man. I belatedly learned that scotch and oysters don't mix. I prefer oysters.

Now, I immediately approached Tim, the erstwhile object of my projectile to thank him for overlooking that incident enough to confirm our membership. When he saw me coming, he looked startled, probably fearful of a repeat performance, I thought.

"Hi Tim! I just want to thank you for the vote of confidence in confirming us as members despite what happened the night we met!" I said smiling broadly, feeling validated.

"OOOOh...Jane! Nice to see you again! I didn't expect to see you tonight."

"You didn't? Why, I certainly wouldn't have missed this nice New Members' Reception after your special dispensation given my social 'faux pas.'"

The reception was, in fact, very pleasant, consisting of delicious complimentary hors d'oeuvres, drinks and welcoming faces. Ironically, during the whole reception I remained blissfully oblivious to the fact that I was now committing yet another 'faux pas,' by just being there.

Even later that evening when we learned that "by tradition the new members' reception didn't include spouses," Dave and I *still* didn't get the implication that the club was for all intents and purposes a men's club.

Prudently, the club had abolished blatant sexist language in its by-laws during the early 1970's. Women could, and occasionally did, become members, but those single women who actually became members were widows of men who had been the member or unmarried women, that is, women who simply could not join as "spouses of members." A special membership was created for them called the Women's Golfing Membership, which offered golfing privileges for much less money but eliminated voting rights. This membership syphoned off most potential female voters.

Married women were strategically called "spouses of members," not "wives of members" which might possibly have alerted people to the reality of the almost total absence of female members. These women had no rights, only "privileges," which by definition were granted by someone else and thus could just as easily be taken away by someone else—as in divorce and death of the member, they routinely were. Women and children were—generally speaking—on a par at the Maple Bluff Country Club except that male children actually had more privileges than their mothers! Sons, even little boys, could enter the Grille Room, while their mothers could not, except one night a week when accompanied by a male adult member. Mothers sent their sons into the Grille Room to get a message to their husbands while they obediently waited outside.

My epiphany that I was not a member came with the realization that the land on which the club sat was public land rented to the private club corporation. As such the property should be used for the equal benefit of all the citizens, not in a discriminatory way against the women.

*

It was 1989, a couple of years since the mailing list had been resolved. I wrote a short note to the country club "suggesting" that it was time to make the Grille Room co-ed. I chose to target the segregated Grille Room because it represented the most blatant and easily remedied exclusion of women. As a reflection of its acquaintance with my resolve in the village mailing list lawsuit, the club agreed to abolish the men-only Grille Room and rename it "The Sports Lounge" making it a co-ed, casual, dining venue. I was delighted. This was an easy victory. I was feeling powerful and gratified...but I was in for a surprise.

About 6 months after the integration of the Grille Room my three daughters and I spent a brutally hot Thursday afternoon at the pool. At the end of the day we decided to avoid returning to the heat of our un-air-conditioned, brick home and instead eat dinner in the air-conditioned Sports Lounge. Because we were coming from the pool clad in sports clothes, our hair still damp, the casual "Sports Lounge" was the perfect place for us. As we changed out of our bathing suits in the women's locker room I commented to my daughters: "Isn't this nice, kids? Now we can go inside and eat in air conditioning even though we won't be formally dressed. If I hadn't lobbied for this, we'd have to go home to eat or go home and change into dressy clothes for the Main Dining Room." I felt pleased to be able to make the point that my work had yielded the benefits to us that the men had always enjoyed. They seemed aware and proud.

Not seeing a host or hostess at the Lounge door, we walked directly in and chose a table for the four of us. Suddenly, seemingly from out of the very walls themselves, a host of personnel appeared at our table: waitresses, the hostess, the bartender, the Assistant Manager, the Manager, surrounded us:

"Excuse me Mrs. Barry, but you cannot eat in here!"

"WHAT?" I said, befuddled. The girls turned quizzically to me wondering what was happening.

"I'm sorry, Mrs. Barry, but it is MEN'S NIGHT tonight."

My middle child, Lydia, 7 at the time, and without any self-censoring, boldly informed the Manager:

"My mother will fix this."

Incredulous, mother tried to do just that; I challenged the accuracy of their assertion: "Yes, but hasn't that been changed? Isn't this the "Sports Lounge" now, not the Men's Grille?"

"Yes, Mrs. Barry, but on Thursdays, the men who golf have exclusive use of the 'Sports Lounge', as they do of the golf course."

Now I got it. There must have been a hullabaloo about the integration of the Grille so backsliding had occurred. Unbeknownst to me, six short months after the announcement that the men's "Grille Room" was integrated and transformed into the "Sports Lounge", there had been a change in the clubhouse rules, reinstating the "men only" tradition on Thursdays, historically men's day on the golf course. Two steps forward, one back.

Despite Lydia's expectations, for the moment there was nothing I could do about it short of engaging in a sit-in right then and there. Instead, frustrated, irritated and humiliated, we docilely followed the manager to the main dining room where there were no gender restrictions, but where there *was* a strictly enforced, formal dress code. In our rumpled sports clothes and damp hair, we sat, self-consciously, surrounded by "perfect people," coiffed and wearing their Sunday best.

Even at 7 years old Lydia was a 'fashionista.' She didn't like being in the formal room dressed informally. Sitting next to me, she whispered:

"Mom, why do they want us to eat in the dining room? We aren't dressed right!"

"Well, they have changed the rules, Lydia. Women and girls are no longer allowed in the Sports Lounge on Thursday nights. We are allowed in the main dining room, so we have to eat in here."

"But Mom, everybody's looking at us because we aren't dressed right."

"I know, Lil, but this is the way they want it, so we will just have to go along with it for now."

At lunch the next day I prepared to address head on the discrimination at the Sacred Cow, the Club. I reasoned that the discriminatory practices at the club all originated from the fact that the membership was almost 100% male. That morning I wrote a letter to the board of the club enumerating the discriminatory practices: the membership categories and practices that discouraged full female membership, the all-male board, the unequal facilities, the unequal tee times, the male-only day in the Sports Lounge, and I suggested that the rules for membership needed to be changed so that women could contribute to policy decisions.

I made a lunch date at the club with my friend, Revan. As she approached the table where I waited, I observed her. As usual she was perfection personified: dignified, aristocratic looking, statuesque at 5'10," her short, silver gray hair perfectly coiffed. She was wearing a classic open collar champagne colored, silk shirt with breast patch pockets and long sleeves. Her tailored skirt was a beige tweed A line, modestly revealing only the last foot or so of her long, slim legs. I felt intensely the distance

I'd come from the two-flat on Bow Street, Arlington, Massachusetts—across the street from the railroad tracks. Revan definitely came from the right side of the tracks. She had grown up in country clubs. Everything about her from her beautiful teeth—I have learned that wealthy people rarely have bad teeth—to her finely tailored suit, to the glint of the gold prep school signet ring on her baby finger, wreaked of privilege. I admired her sophistication. Her friendship confirmed my own socio-economic success.

I had enlisted her opinion about the mailing list and retained her friendship, but how far could she be pushed before she bailed on me? I was nervous about blowing my good fortune by raising the topic of sex discrimination again with her. *Aren't I fortunate enough, coming from where I came from, to be in her company, to have risen socially to a point where she is my friend? All my efforts as a youngster to do well in school, the financial struggles to pay for college, the challenge of the Ph.D., the painstaking efforts to build my real estate business, for what? To reach financial and social success.* I could hear my mother's voice inside me saying, "What are you doing introducing a topic that might alienate Revan and jeopardize your friendship?"

With every break in the conversation, I thought about the topic I was about to introduce, but hesitated, afraid she would think me rabid, someone to avoid. After all, she had initially considered the issue of the village's all-male mailing list inconsequential. It was only after her *husband* agreed with me that she could appreciate its significance. So, I knew her inclination was as mine had always been: to minimize, to ignore, to deny discrimination.

But, the Fates were at work. Don Sweet appeared in our line of vision. A brand-new member of the club, he had just been nominated to serve on the Board of Directors. He had boyish good looks, was the proverbial, ingratiating, glad hand, pressing the flesh of several as he made his way to his table. If there were babies available, he would have kissed them. I took his appearance as a sign. It provided a natural segue to the forbidden topic. I took a deep inhale and began gingerly:

"Revan, did you see that Don Sweet is one of the nominees for the Board of Directors of the Club?"

"Yes, I did! *Who the heck is he*, anyway? I've never even *heard* of the guy before!"

"Oh," I said, beginning with forced casualness, "the Sweets live near me. He's the brother of the Sweets who used to live across the street from you—but my feelings exactly!"

I was encouraged that she didn't even know him.

I continued: "He only joined the club a year or so ago. What's he doing as a board nominee is my question. Why are they putting some unknown man up when they could be nominating their first woman, YOU, a person who has served the club so loyally for so many years?"

"Oh, Jane, that's nice of you, but I don't have to be nominated to the board. What does it matter?"

I pressed on. "Well, Revan, I just thought that since you have been willing to serve on so many committees of the club when you aren't even a member, you might like to serve on the board to encourage the club to make wives members."

There was no backing out now. I had opened the forbidden door.

"What do you mean that *I'm not a member*? I am too a member! Why, I've been a member for years and years!"

"No, Revan, you may *think* you're a member. You attend everything, including committee meetings, as if you *are* a member, but the truth is you *aren't* one. Only Bill is the member. As his wife you have privileges at the club but no rights. So, you see, you've been serving on committees of a club of which you aren't even a member! Strange, huh?"

Her jaw dropped, a furrow appeared on her forehead: "Is that *really* right?"

I nodded and continued to lobby:

"When there are no women on the board, when women are not part of the policy making process, we aren't part of the power. How can we be? We aren't even members! Revan, I think that we ought to be members, don't you? We participate in club activities all the time. Actually, we do a lot of the grunt work. We should have a say in how things are run...a vote at the very least, *especially* since the land upon which the club is situated is public land, land owned by ALL the citizens of the village, female citizens as well as male citizens. Such a publicly held property should not be used in a discriminatory manner."

"Well...yes...I suppose that's so."

I pressed on, finding more confidence the more I spoke: "That way, Revan, people like you who have worked so many years will have an opportunity to serve on the board—if you wish. I've written a letter to the board making these very points. Will you help me make some of these changes?"

As it happened, Revan, a friend of hers, whose help I also solicited, and I ended up lobbying the club's president and its board. It took about a year's worth of meetings and letters, but eventually the board begrudgingly agreed to our proposal that women (euphemistically referred to as "spouses") become full members like their husbands. In the fall of 1989 wives of golfing members (the golfing membership was the most exclusive of the various membership classes and the only one with voting rights) were accorded equal membership rights with their husbands. Revan, and another woman, the Vice-President and part owner of a national manufacturing company headquartered in Madison, were nominated and confirmed to be the first two females on the Board of Directors.

I was thrilled. The all-male dining room/bar had been eliminated—except on Thursdays, men's golf day—and now wives of Regular or Golfing members were members in their own right and two were serving as board members, able to change policy.

CHAPTER 18

The night of Revan's installation as a member of the club's board I called to congratulate her and revel with her in our achievement. There was no answer at her house that night or for several days thereafter. I heard belatedly that the very night of the installation she left on a private jet for the Palm Springs, California residence of the national manufacturing company's owner. One of that company's executives, a man who had previously demonstrated his lack of enthusiasm for any changes to club rules to promote women's equality in the club, was the newly installed President of The Maple Bluff Country Club. The female co-owner of the company was the other woman installed as a club board member with Revan. I conjectured that as co-owners of a large company, she and her husband wanted no more trouble for the club—or by association, for their company—from my friend as she assumed her new duties as a Director.

Shortly after the installation I wrote another letter to the newly co-ed board asking that the remaining discriminatory practices (like the men-only day in the Sports Lounge that my daughters and I had innocently encountered), the gender restrictions on the golf course and driving range and the inequities in the club's amenities, be abolished.

Despite my entreaties, very little was done to eliminate the remaining issues. Even Revan, who was independently wealthy and therefore had no financial constraints on her feminist activities, backed away from making further changes. Every time I saw her after her installation as a board member she either avoided the subject of the club altogether or lamented how difficult it was to make changes.

"Jane, *we've made our point.* Progress has been made. The club is acting in good faith. It's changing its ways. To criticize now would amount to betrayal of their good faith."

Our friendship was strained by my expectations and her hesitation. I had thought that by getting women into positions of power, the remaining discrepancies between the rights and privileges afforded men and women would be addressed. Now, I realized that I could not count on Revan to work from the inside on these issues. It wasn't that she didn't see the discrimination or want it eliminated. She simply didn't want to endure the repercussions of standing up to it any more.

One of the last times I spoke at any length with her after her installation to office, she had been humiliated. I stopped by her house hoping to chat about club developments. She told me that against all tradition the club President had just unilaterally appropriated to himself the right to appoint the Chair of the Committee over which she was to preside as Director. When she told me the situation, outraged, I urged her to resist:

"Tell him you object! Tell him that it's your right and responsibility to appoint your own Chair for your Committee. Who does he think he is appropriating your authority?"

"I know, Jane," she said in a tired and dejected voice.

"Well, don't let him get away with it, Revan!" I persisted.

I was frustrated. She held a position on the board, yes, but she was like the daughter dressing up in grown-up's clothes. While all the male Directors always chose their own committee chairs, my friend suffered in silence with the President's choice, one of his male cronies. She wasn't assuming equal authority with the men on the board.

By being silent about continued sexist attitudes and practices, she simply became an "exception" when she served on the board. Her presence implicitly endorsed the impression that the club no longer discriminated against women when in fact, despite some changes, the club remained discriminatory. The difference now was that she *participated* in implementing its discriminatory policies. While it took 66.67% of the board to ratify any proposal, there was a 'de facto' quota of 20-30% women allowed

176

on the board at any one time. Consequently, "eternal daughterhood", was still in effect. Until women board members asserted equal adulthood and demanded that there be equal representation for women on the powerful committees, the presence of women on the club board—or any other board for that matter—was no sign of real change. Instead, it amounted to collusion.

*

Dave, a classicist by training, coined a term for us women, who rise in the predominantly male power structure only to condone and to implement discrimination against ourselves and other women. He calls us 'patronae', "women who do the dirty work for the patriarchy." For him we are reminiscent of a common, if not stock, character of Roman comedy, (see Terence's *The Eunuch*) the pompous wife, who thinks she is powerful and important, but who unwittingly presides over her own and other women's abuse.

The Latin word 'patrona' is the feminine of 'patronus', or patron, the truly powerful male who like a father rules by reward (patrimony) and punishment. The 'patrona' *thinks* she is powerful like the 'patronus' while in reality she has been "patronized", bought off with an empty token, so that she implements the patronus' will. Ironically, as "token" women rise in the hierarchy and act as 'patronae', women who would attack the discriminatory system are forced to attack fellow women. As Gerda Lerner states: "The system of patriarchy can function only with the cooperation of women."

*

I continued to write to Revan and the rest of the board asking that they take action until finally I realized that the only way to effect further change was through coercion. In June of 1990 at my request the ACLU

177

agreed to support my efforts to confront the continued sexist practices at Maple Bluff Country Club. Threatening a suit, we coerced the board to abolish the restrictions on women's use of the Sports Lounge and the driving range and to eliminate the male only weekend hours that excluded women from play. Further, a rule that membership in the club automatically went to the husband in the case of a divorce was amended to state that it went "to the person so designated in the divorce decree." The club also agreed "to consider" enlarging and upgrading the women's locker facilities to allow access to beverage and dining service similar to that enjoyed in the men's locker room. To accomplish these changes no lawsuit was necessary, simply the ACLU's letter that without change I would be a plaintiff in court, again. They were much more cooperative this time around.

At the expiration of the two women's terms on the board, the club bulletin arrived in our mailbox announcing the election of two more women board members. I settled down to read with satisfaction their biographies. Immediately, I was bewildered. Both women were described as "long time members of the club:" one a member for 10 years; the other for 20 years.

What's going on? Oh, my God, the club must have concocted these bios to obliterate the fact that both of the women have been members for only 3 years, the length of time that has elapsed since I and my two friends successfully lobbied to amend the bylaws so that "spouses of members" (wives) can be equal members with their husbands. Is this a case of the club re-writing history, concealing facts, concocting its own version of things?

I was shocked at the thought that the club would be so boldly duplicitous as to present the women as long-time members when they weren't.

It was March of 1991, "Women's History Month." I decided to raise this historical inaccuracy with the woman who had been designated the "20-year member." We were acquainted and I believed that she would be sympathetic to the issue because of an earlier incident.

She and her husband had invited Dave and me to a huge open house party to celebrate the completion of their palatial, new lakeside home with its indoor pool and racquetball court. This was one of our very few invitations that year. At that party she had commented to me, perhaps aware of my feminist activities, that the house really wasn't hers, but rather her husband's, because she had made only one request when it was being designed—that it have a linen closet. There was no linen cupboard anywhere in the mammoth home.

Given her careful definition of the house as "his", I expected her to be sensitive and responsive to my similar attempt to set the record straight regarding the country club membership. Before she had attended on "his," her husband's, membership. Now she, like all wives, was a member in her own right.

So, I called her up to see if she, too, had noticed the glaring error in the article about her. She promptly responded: "You mean the part about my being a 20-year member?"

"Yes! So, you noticed that too, Helen?!" I was delighted to think that she too recognized the transformation of 'her-story' into 'his-story.' Just as I was basking in the warmth of a kindred spirit's camaraderie, to my disbelief, she responded:

"Of course, I noticed it. I wrote it!"

Confounded, hardly able to believe what I was hearing, I could only manage a weak: "Wha...Wha...Whyyyy, if you realized that it's not accurate, did you write it?"

"I...I felt like it."

It was no wonder she felt like it. She was supposed to do this: ignore the fact that she and all the other women had not really been members all those years and justify her qualifications to sit on the board via her long term "membership."

"But Helen, I can't tell you how painful it is to me that the actual situation is not represented accurately. It has been such a struggle to obtain membership rights for women. To accomplish it has cost me dearly both socially and professionally; without my fight you and Glynn would not be on the board, nor would you be able to vote. I mean neither of you would even be members of the club for God's sake! You would simply be 'the spouses of a member' as you have been for the last twenty years! Only your husbands would have the right to participate in club governance."

Beyond expressing my own pain at a whitewashing of the situation, I admitted to her my own collusion: "Helen, I spent the first 38 years of my life not seeing, but instead minimizing, ignoring and denying sex discrimination. By doing so I never did anything to correct the situation. I allowed discrimination to continue uncontested. To change things, I had to face reality, call a spade a spade. In order to make progress it's critical that we acknowledge discrimination, past and present and stand up to it. Will you please consider submitting a correction to the article to set the record straight."

In a flat voice with no affect, she said: "I am busy, Jane. I've got to go."

The next thing I heard was the even flatter dial tone.

*

In 1992 I wrote a letter to the President of the Club, a lawyer, objecting to the revisionist history perpetrated in the newly installed female board members' bios. He published my letter in the monthly club newsletter as a 'corrigendum'. Ironically, instead of an indictment of the club's long-standing history of discrimination, my letter revealed the female coverup of it!

CHAPTER 19

"Mom, you'll never guess what happened yesterday!"

"What?"

"Well, you know Kristin, the little friend of Lydia's, who lives down the hill from us?"

"Yes. What about her?"

"Well, she had a birthday party yesterday and Lydia wasn't even invited. I'm thinking it was because her parents object to my activism."

"Jane, what do you expect? Who do you think you are anyway? Of course, the villagers will resent some newcomer telling them how to run their village and their club. You move into their community and criticize them."

"Well, Mom, I didn't just move into their community yesterday. I've lived here for 10 years without criticizing a thing. I happen to have discovered things that really need changing. Do you think it's right that only the men in a municipality should receive governmental notices of elections, legal matters, matters effecting all the citizens—that government owned land should be rented to a club that discriminates against its female citizens? You know that's what's been happening here. When I realized it, I tried to address it quietly, amicably, but it didn't work."

"Jane, you are a fool and wrong to boot to challenge the establishment. In the first place the women won't thank you and in the second place, of course, you are going to rile people up and cause repercussions for yourself and your kids. I mean, I hate to say this, Jane, but if I lived in Maple Bluff, I would be on the other side. "

I'd been mindlessly cleaning the kitchen counters as I talked on the phone, but now I stopped at that statement. I couldn't say a word. That was a painful and incredible thought, that my own mother would actually be on the other side if she lived in my community. She wouldn't be my ally. She wouldn't even be neutral. She would be my opponent in my stand for the dignity of equal treatment by the village government and the country club.

All the talk during my childhood about my being the equal of anyone, man or woman, had been forgotten. If my stand for equal adulthood with my father foreshadowed what I would face from other men, then my experience with my mother mirrored what I was facing from most other women (myself included) when I objected to male supremacy.

I should have been prepared for her reaction. When I had declared independence, Dad had reacted angrily, insisting that he stay in our home. When I didn't intercede between him and Dave when he didn't abide by my instructions to come to my office if they arrived in town early, he considered his paternal relationship with me ended. If my mother objected to his attitude, if she felt his reactions were overbearing, irrational or unwarranted, she never let on. She never distanced herself from his stance. Instead she was silent. This was the pattern that prevailed. She endorsed—if only by her inertia—my father's will and rejection of me for my assertions of equality with him.

Upon reflection, I realized that her own acceptance of "eternal daughterhood" was clear throughout my childhood. Beyond her constant unwarranted inflation of Dad's importance and portrayal of herself as his inferior—a situation which always discomforted me because I sensed the fraudulence of it—there were blatant incidents like her single-handedly getting my father, not herself, elected to the town council.

Mom had an abiding fascination with politics. Well-known in the community and well-versed in issues of public policy, she might have won office herself, but typical of the era, she deferred to Dad. He was likable enough but not the type for political office. Basically, he was somewhat introverted and while he had firmly held opinions on matters of public policy, Dad had little inclination to take political action. He wasn't averse to the honor of being an elected official though he would rather be woodworking or tinkering with his car—and my mother was willing to do the work to make him one. In the end he was Ron McCall, a town council member, a Selectman—of all things—and she, she was "*Mrs.* Ronald H. McCall, wife of a Selectman." This was as close as she got to a political position.

Because my mother's idealization of Dad bore little resemblance to the real man and because her claims of inferiority to him were so incredible, even as a child I sensed the extent of the game they played. That game never changed. What changed as I aged was my mother's eventual and inevitable application of the rules of female conduct and subordination to me, the would-be "exception."

When I was growing up, she displayed a feminist spirit in her admiration of me, her daughter, in her pride in my abilities and accomplishments, her hopes for my future, her objection to my playing second fiddle to any of my male peers. Even in my teenage years it was she who always encouraged me to continue in math and science like the boys, not to opt out like most girls. But now she was not supportive or proud of me as I demanded equal status with men in general and with Dad in particular.

Early evidence of the change in my mother's attitude toward me was her negative reaction to my doctoral ambitions in 1970, but there was more. When my father was sullen and irritated by what he perceived as our short stay of several days at his 65th birthday, feeling that he had been "sandwiched" into other plans that Dave and I had, Mom was totally silent. Her silence was more significant than I realized at the time. At that point I hadn't fully realized the gravity of my transgressions—my sins of claiming equality and independence. Subliminally I knew that I had shirked my filial obligations to Dad by considering my own life and plans as important as his, but I didn't realize my mother's stance.

If I was wrong to assert equality with my father, my mother also felt that I was wrong to oppose the established authorities in Maple Bluff and the country club. My mother, as well as my father, disagreed vehemently with my stand. Not far beneath the surface of her criticisms of my active feminism in Wisconsin was the connection between it and my declaration of equality with Dad. Both actions violated my father's will, his appropriate authority and therefore the principle of eternal daughterhood. I was a woman and "they" were men like my father but that truth was never uttered. Just as democratic principles didn't apply to me as a daughter in the family, so they were irrelevant in the outside world.

Having lived through the trauma of her own family's financial demise in the Great Depression, Mom had always been pragmatic. With her eye constantly on the bottom line, she would not, personally, pursue an ideal with a financial risk, but her disapproval of my position stunned me. She considered me a fool for championing women's rights when other women, who would have certainly benefited from my successful efforts, hung back.

Intellectually, she may have agreed with me about sexism but the issue was coming too close to home. Espousal of my cause would necessitate a treachery against my father who rejected my Maple Bluff actions. In most of my conversations with her from 1984 on, I either avoided the subject of my feminist efforts in order to keep the peace or attempted unsuccessfully to convert her.

Dad rarely voiced his objection to my activism; it wasn't necessary. Mom did that for him, but in the fall of 1988 he did so unequivocally himself. I had recently emerged victorious from my encounter with the village over the mailing list when my parents came to Madison for another one of their, by now, infamous visits. One evening we dined out at a local restaurant. The atmosphere was already tense because Dave and I had attended a "going away" cocktail party for a friend of ours prior to the dinner hour. Thus, my parents had had to wait for our return.

During dinner, the subject of my lawsuit against the village arose. My father commented: "I've never understood why you were so upset about this mailing list thing anyway?" I explained for the umpteenth time that the omission of women on the mailing list embodied the village's practice of treating the males in a household as primary, as the official, but unelected, representatives of the females in each household. I told him that I was opposed to my government's institutionalization in its official mailing list of the sexist attitude that men were the "heads of their households" and as such should be the politically active ones while women should be the ones they represent.

When he trivialized the significance of the issue, I bit.

I recalled the town council episode where my mother got him elected to a position she was much more qualified to hold because convention mandated that women stay in the background. When he realized that I was criticizing their gender-based roles and their acceptance of its fraudulence, he said: "I've had enough of this. Come on, Peg. Let's get out of here." He got up and walked out of the restaurant leaving us sitting at the table...with the bill.

My mother followed him.

To join me in my opposition to the village's mailing list or the sexist practices at the country club would have required Mom's public repudiation of the premise of the primacy of men in their households. Specifically, it would have required repudiation of her own husband's supremacy in their household. Ultimately, she would be rejecting their relationship, a relationship based on hierarchy, the artificial elevation of Dad and the artificial subordination of her. She'd been married for more than forty years. Her stake in the 'status quo' was huge. She was unwilling to change even if on the village list, at the country club and in my own family, men were elevated simply because they were men.

In retrospect, I realize that my mother prophesied her behavior. When my sister and I were just girls at home in Arlington, we got into a discussion with Mom. It took place in our dining room when I was about 12 and my sister 9. I don't know what precipitated it, but it involved the question of where one's loyalties lie, with one's children or with one's spouse. Mom was a very caring and conscientious mother, but I remember being shocked when she categorically declared: "Well, I must admit, girls, that if it came down to a choice between my children and my husband, I would always choose your father."

Shocked, I pressed:

"Really, Mom?! You wouldn't choose us?"

Very matter-of-factly, even adamantly, she responded:

"No. Your father is my mate for life. My marriage vows are forever, 'For better for worse, in sickness and in health till death do us part.' You girls are only around for a short while. I love you dearly, but your father is my lifetime mate."

I was both comforted and alarmed by her words: comforted by my parents' dependable, secure bond. They were devoted to one another, rarely argued, were indeed partners for life. With their marriage they had created a stable and serene environment for us, but I felt loss and shock too. I was not her priority. We were not her priority. She had pledged her fealty to my father.

In fact, Dad had rescued her. He had rescued her from the humiliation of being "unchosen". Although she was 18 or 19 when they met in 1941, my mother had had few dates and had recently endured the excruciating pain of not being invited to her own senior prom. The prospect of being "an old maid," not selected to be one of the protected ones, loomed large for her until my father's advent. As a child, dependent on her, I had never recognized that she was actually a dependent herself and as such had a loyalty that competed with her loyalty to her daughters.

Family lore communicated through her sister, my Aunt May, has it that on the night of her senior prom in 1940 some neighborhood friends of my grandparents visited unexpectedly. When my mother realized that they would see that she had not been invited, she dashed in embarrassment and humiliation into my grandparents' bedroom, crouching in disgrace and fear of discovery, in a corner of their small, cluttered closet. She remained there until the company left—several hours later. She couldn't bear the thought that anyone would know she had not been "chosen." The gods—men—had spurned her. Without their approval she could not face the world. Her sense of self-worth depended on it.

In exchange for her reverence for my father, her idealization of him, she received his male 'imprimatur' and his financial support, a necessity in a world in which she was ill equipped to support herself. She would not risk that to join me in my battle against the male establishment in Maple Bluff, Wisconsin. She knew the pain of rejection by men. She was grateful that my father had rescued her from further such indignities.

I understood the genesis, but that didn't obliterate the sense of betrayal, my disappointment and confusion at my mother's reaction to my stand for equal rights.

CHAPTER 20

As my father lay dying of prostate cancer, in 1993, he stretched his hand weakly towards me and whispered, "I love you, Janie."

"I love you too, Dad."

Everything else important remained unsaid. We weren't mentioning his impending death. Even in the face of death, he wouldn't admit to me that he was dying. I didn't know for sure if he admitted it to himself. But the recent animosity between us didn't matter now. My struggle for authority over my own life; his angry response. That struggle was done. All that remained was love.

We never said goodbye.

I had tried to introduce the subject of his death over a year earlier in December of '91 when Dad was still in reasonably good condition but his bone scan had revealed what he described as *an irritation*. The doctors were going to monitor this *bone irritation*. He kept talking about *irritations*. I kept trying to talk about cancer.

About a month after the bone metastasis was discovered as I was driving my children and husband through the Everglades in a rented van. Suddenly I could barely see the road through my tears. Instead, I saw my Mom and Dad thirty years earlier in robust health driving this very same stretch in their green '57 Ford Fairlane, with my sister and me playing happily in the back seat. Now despite his unwillingness to discuss it, my Dad was back in Massachusetts, dying.

That night I woke up in our rented condo in Naples, Florida at 2:30 A.M. and spent the rest of the night writing him a letter. In it I acknowledged that I was aware that the new medical report about the bone involvement meant we probably didn't have much time left. I quoted the

Jim Croce lyrics that had prompted my tears that afternoon: *"I would give anything I own, give up my life, my heart, my home. I would give anything I own just to have you back again."* and told him that despite our differences I wanted him to know that I loved him and thanked him for being a sincere and caring dad.

As I stood at the mailbox the next morning with the letter in my hand, I must have appeared to be suffering a fit of paralysis or perhaps Parkinson's. I had trouble releasing the letter from my grasp. Once I dropped it in the box, I couldn't retrieve it, couldn't stop it from making its inexorable way to my father. I was talking to my father about *his death.* Even alluding to his vulnerability was breaking the code of silence he was imposing, but I felt it was important to seize the moment, to communicate before it was forever too late.

We returned home to Wisconsin from Florida and I waited for a call from him, a letter—something, anything. Several weeks passed with no response. Then in early February I learned that another scan had shown that the "irritation" was growing. He was to undergo an orchiectomy— removal of the testicles—in order to inhibit the hormonally induced growth of the cancer. The exact date for the operation wasn't set yet. I told him that I would be there for the operation. He said it wasn't necessary, but since I knew the orchiectomy meant the disease itself was inoperable, I insisted I would come.

It wasn't until late the afternoon of the day before the operation was to occur that I finally got word of its date and time. It was taking place early *the very next morning.* The logistics to make it to Boston from Madison in time were daunting, but I was committed to being there before Dad went under the anesthetic. This was the first operation I had ever known Dad to undergo. For all I knew, he might never emerge alive.

Everything happened so fast; I found myself on a plane at 9:30 P.M. that evening with $15 in my wallet. When I arrived at Logan Airport in Boston at 11 P.M. I had just enough taxi money to get to my Aunt and

Uncle's house outside Harvard Square in Cambridge. The next morning my uncle drove me to the hospital in Arlington.

It was 7:30 A.M. when I asked the hospital receptionist for help to locate Dad. She directed me to the floor where the operating rooms were located, informing me that I might be able to find him in one of the "prep" rooms. I hurried to the nearest stairwell taking the steps two at a time to the third floor. I ran down the hall ducking my head into every open doorway until I found Dad. He was lying on a gurney, covered in a white sheet with a nurse by his side attempting to start an intravenous tube.

Disheveled and out of breath, I collected myself as best I could, smiled and said brightly:

"Hey, Dad! Here I am. I'm so glad I made it before you went in!"

He didn't exactly bound up and hug me. Only the suggestion of a smile came across his face. I figured he was uneasy to have me witness his present vulnerability or maybe, he was under sedation. In any case, I pressed on: "How are you doing?"

In a tone that seemed to express irritation at such a stupid question when he was about to have his testicles removed, he said quickly: "I'm doing just fine."

Then he pointed to the nurse standing next to him. "Mary Ann, here, is taking good care of me."

I heard: '...better care of me than some people I know.'

"What are you doing here anyway? Why aren't you home with your mother and Kathryn?"

This was the first I learned that my mother and sister weren't at the hospital. I assumed that I would be meeting them there. I was stunned to learn that they were at home.

"I thought for sure Mom and Kathryn would be here, Dad!"

At that, my father said brusquely: "Well, they're not. They're waiting at home, Jane. There's no reason to come here. Why don't you go home and stay with them."

191

I had just flown half way across the country to be at the hospital before he went into surgery. Rationally, I knew there was nothing I could do to make his operation any safer, but somehow, it only seemed right for me to be there in the building before, during, and after he came out. I tried to ignore the edge to his voice:

"Well, to be honest, Dad, I don't have any money on me to get a cab home. I wasn't worried because I was going to be meeting Mom and Kathryn here. Anyway, it'll be good luck for you to have a friend here—right?"

Instead of warming to my assurance that he'd have 'a friend' waiting for him, he once again pointed to his nurse and with no hint of a smile stated matter-of-factly: "I already have a friend. *She's* my friend."

I was stunned by his frosty behavior, by the implication that I wasn't his "friend." The poor nurse seemed uncomfortable and embarrassed too. Trying to smooth the situation she jovially suggested: "You can never have too many friends, Mr. McCall."

With that chance at an honorable retreat, I said "That's right, Dad. I love you!" Then I pecked him on the cheek and withdrew to a waiting room.

After the operation when Dad was home and we were alone, I asked him: "Dad, did you ever receive the letter I sent you from the Everglades a while back?"

He paused, seemed to be struggling to remember. Then he turned to me and looked me dead in the eye: "Oh, yuh, I got that...but I didn't 'get it.'"

His tone told me that the matter was closed. He would not speak about his death.

That was all he ever said about my attempt to relate as two loved ones confronting imminent death. I wanted to share my sadness with him. I wanted to dispense with the roles before there was no more opportunity. If he remained the invincible, superman there would be no chance of really connecting. He would just pretend to be strong and then die—forever.

I stayed at my parents' home in Arlington for several days after his operation. The atmosphere in the house was tense, subdued, gloomy. No one wanted to talk about it, but Dad had been castrated. There was a heavy sense of loss permeating the place. I attributed Dad's irritability in the hospital before the operation and his refusal to relate to my letter to his difficulty dealing with the orchiectomy.

The operation took place in February of '92. For about nine months afterwards, the strategy to attack the cancer's spread by blocking any hormonal stimulation of the tumor seemed to be working. Dad returned to apparent good health. I kept in touch by regular phone calls and visited that summer.

Then in November the bone scans showed the cancer had begun to grow again. This was very unexpected because we all thought that the orchiectomy and consequent lowering of the testosterone levels would serve to put the cancer into a much longer remission. Dad assured me that the doctor still had "lots of tricks up his sleeve." They were going to start him on chemotherapy. At this news, I decided to call his oncologist directly. I needed to know the prognosis.

Was there a possibility of a cure or another remission? How sick would he be during the treatment? Would it be wise for me to come immediately? Was the chemotherapy a sign that he was dying?

It wasn't easy, but I finally made direct phone contact with his doctor. I had the feeling that it was very irregular for a daughter to be calling her father's doctor directly, and long distance to boot, to inquire about her dad's condition. I worried that I was violating my father's privacy; that the doctor wouldn't share confidential information with me; that he would consider me completely out of line. Still, once the doctor had told me that the chemotherapy was palliative, that it could possibly prolong life but not effect a cure, I went right to the heart of the matter:

"How much time does my father have, Dr. Anderson?" I asked

forthrightly, but totally unprepared for the answer.

"About six months. Maybe less."

I was sitting in my office, pen in hand, ready to be efficient, to take notes knowing that in these emotionally charged situations, one often forgets what isn't written in black and white for future reference. I was prepared for the usual ambiguity: 'Oh, it's difficult to tell in these matters. Why some people respond so well to the chemotherapy, they recover completely. Others...' I wasn't prepared for an emphatic: "six month— maybe less." The tension passed out of my body with a sigh. The pen fell out of my hand. I had known Dad was in bad shape —*but only six months to live—or LESS? How could this be?* Dad hadn't said anything to me about it. He didn't even look that sick.

"Does Dad know this?!" I asked, almost shrieking with shock.

Quietly, the doctor answered: "I don't know."

That answer floored me.

Incredulous at what I was hearing, I challenged him: "You don't know?! Well, haven't you *told* him?"

The doctor was becoming defensive. "No, I haven't. He's never asked that question."

None of my family knew that Dad had at most six months to live. No one—not my mother, not my sister, not her husband, Peter. For God's sake, not even my father! Only I knew, because only I had asked. And according to the doctor, this ignorance might be for the best—medically. It was his opinion that sometimes bad news caused worse response to the treatment. Thus, I was left alone with a terrible secret.

Over the next six months I called frequently and visited once in January with plans to return in May for his 75th birthday. By January he had a shunt implanted in his chest to administer the chemotherapy twenty-four hours a day. It may have been my awareness of the shunt, but his eyes looked tired and he appeared frail. When I asked how he felt he admitted to feeling "Waaabd oot," his expression culled from his years in the Navy, I think, for "wiped out." He explained that the chemotherapy was destroying the red blood cells which carry energizing oxygen throughout the body. Dad always liked to understand the mechanics of phenomena. It seemed to give him a sense of control I think.

During this period, I walked a tight rope, trying to talk about his disease in a way that treated it seriously without directly stating what I knew, that he was in the final months of his life. I desperately wanted him to enter himself in a clinical trial at one of the world-renowned research facilities in Boston because I knew that the standard treatment he was receiving was futile, palliative at best. Without telling him the truth—that he had so little time—my ideas seemed extreme. I used the internet and a contact I had at the University of Wisconsin-Madison to locate what seemed a promising new treatment for advanced metastatic prostate cancer, but ultimately, although he went to meet with the doctor administering the testing, Dad declined the program. He wanted to give the chemotherapy he was already on 'a chance to do its thing'.

*

Now as he lay dying in Arlington's local Symmes Hospital I had a choice. He had a very short time to live. I knew that. I felt it. A matter of days. The doctors said otherwise. "A month, maybe more," they assured me when I pressed them for some sense of the situation. My two younger daughters, Lydia, 11, and Margaret, 9, were impatiently awaiting my return to Madison, but if the doctors thought Dad's death was imminent, I would certainly stay in Arlington longer. Instead, the doctors were suggesting my mother investigate Hospice for when the hospital released him to her care.

Do I follow my gut that says that he has only a few days and stick around for the end? Or do I take the easy way out, base my decision on the doctors' predictions and leave for a while? I can always come back if Dad wants me or needs me...but why would he need me? I'm no doctor. He'd only need me if he wanted to tell me he was dying—if he wanted to say "Good-bye, honey."

If I don't stay and he dies without my being here, how will I feel? I won't have another chance to see him. Heck, what does it matter? He isn't ever going to say 'Good-bye' anyway.

I want out—right now.

I had done what I could do under the circumstances. I had expressed my gratitude for all the good he had done, for being a loving dad who provided us with security and affection. I had tried to penetrate his facade, tried to talk about death as two human beings who care deeply for one another and were facing an unimaginable loss, but I had failed. I wasn't going to get what I wanted; I wanted Dad to stop playing the super role.

I felt tired and sad, repulsed by the ugliness of his disease, unalleviated by any real relating. His neck was boney and scrawny, betraying the devastation of the cancer, while his forearms and hands seemed strangely fleshy, fat, inflated—with no muscle tone. They were bloated like one of those grotesque giant floats in the Macy's Thanksgiving Parade—filled with liquid cancer. He was in pain and suffering.

I seized the opportunity to leave for what I knew in my heart would be the last time. Following his lead, I simply said, "I have to go home now, Dad, but I'll come back if you need me."

He nodded and said "Bye, Hon." Tears welled in his tired eyes as I kissed his forehead. The uncharacteristic tears said that he—in his head—as I, in mine,—knew the "Bye" was final, but we both acted as though it was no different from any other parting.

It was an unsatisfying end. I had grown up. I could accept that Dad was human and therefore mortal, but Dad couldn't admit it—at least not to me. He still played Dad. As I walked out into the hospital parking lot, I felt lost and strange. There was no unadulterated sadness, the way it was supposed to be. Instead, there was a part of me that actually felt relieved to be released from the situation...even though I so loved him.

The sun was shining brightly; there was a light, clean, spring breeze. I took off my blazer, tossed it into the back seat, lowered the windows and drove away feeling the clear air streaming through the car.

*

Two days later in Wisconsin, I woke to my sister's call. "Janie? Janie, it's Kathryn. Janie, he's dead. Dad is dead."

CHAPTER 21

Shortly after Dad's death in May of '93, unexpectedly, his will arrived in the mail: "KNOW ALL MEN BY THESE PRESENT that I, Ronald H. McCall...do hereby make and declare this instrument to be my LAST WILL AND TESTAMENT..."

He was declaring to "ALL Men" his intention for his daughters and wife.

I was stunned and devastated. At first I thought I had misread the Will. I read the sentences again but I was having trouble making any sense out of them. They seemed a jumble of unrelated words. My eyes skipped from line to line and back again. When, finally, I realized that what I read was what it really said, I was suffocating. It was as if someone kicked me in the stomach. As I tried to catch my breath, I couldn't. It seemed there was no room in my lungs for any air. All I could do was take sharp, short gasps all the while straining through tears trying to see that I was reading the words wrong. But I was not wrong. My father had left both our childhood homes, the one we were raised in in Arlington and "Manomet," our summer cottage that he had built with his own hands, the houses being the bulk of his estate, to Mom until she died and then only to Kathryn at Mom's death.

The will had been sent by my parents' attorney, a man I knew as a girl when I sang in the Park Avenue Congregational Church choir with him and his wife. I ran to the phone and called him at his office number listed on the cover letter. I hoped that he could offer some explanation to salve the wound. I hadn't seen Bob for 25 years, but I recognized his voice immediately when he answered.

I began composed: "Hi Bob, this is Jane McCall Barry, Ron McCall's daughter."

"Oh, hi Jane! Nice to hear from you. How are you? Good, I hope."

How am I? Terrible!

His question did me in. When I tried to explain how I felt, my voice broke. "Oh, Bob," I wailed. "I just received Dad's Will. Why did Dad disinherit me?"

He gasped: " You mean you didn't know? I...I thought you knew. I thought he had told you, Jane."

"No! I had no idea! Did he tell you why?"

"No. I just got the impression that it was all agreed to."

"No, Bob, Dad never mentioned anything about this to me."

Like me, Bob never would have expected that my father would disinherit me without at least telling me. Bob had no idea of any tension in our relationship.

Now he realized how shocked I was: "Oh, Jane, we've got to get your mother, your sister and you together to iron this thing out."

I had already made plans to visit Mom in August for her 70th birthday. I had bought the plane ticket soon after Dad died at the end of May. This being her first birthday without Dad and such a significant one, I knew it was critical for me to be there with and for her. Bob set the family meeting at her house to coincide with my August visit.

The day of the meeting with the lawyer we were in Mom's dining room, the place of much happier memories. It felt strange to be holding such a meeting there in a place where we celebrated our family harmony, where we each sat so many times as members of a close family. We had never had a business meeting here, only celebratory meals: birthdays, holiday dinners, meals for honored guests. Now Mom took the chair closest to the kitchen where she customarily sat for all our festive dining occasions, so that she could easily replenish food. Ironically, for some subconscious reason I took the seat opposite Mom at the other end of the table, a seat made empty by Dad's absence. We all chatted superficially until Bob raised the subject we were gathered there to discuss.

"Peg, as you know I suggested this meeting when Jane called me and expressed distress at Ron's will. Maybe you want to explain why you and Ron gave the two homes to Kathryn."

So, Mom's will mirrored Dad's? I looked across the table at Mom. Now I could see that she didn't appear remorseful, uncomfortable, embarrassed or conciliatory. Instead, she was looking directly at me, sort of quizzically, her eyebrows somewhat knit over her dark brown eyes, lips pursed and twisted to the left as if she were chewing the inside of her lower right lip. *How is she going to explain my disinheritance? Is she going to condemn my feminism; or tell me that Dad didn't like it that I put them up at the St. Benedict's Center when Margaret was born?'*

Instead of a statement of explanation, she suddenly asked: "Jane, why would you think that we should have given you a share equal to Kathryn's? You haven't even been here to help us while Kathryn always has."

Now I was the one with the knit eyebrows but my lips were not pursed. My mouth was agape. I was astounded, aghast. True, Kathryn had remained all her life in the immediate area, just blocks away from our childhood home and been a dutiful and loving daughter while I had moved out to the Midwest when I was 24, striking out for new territory. Dad (and evidently, Mom, as well) seemed to have taken that geographic distance as symbolic of defection. Now Dad's behavior at the hospital the day of his orchiectomy made sense: "I have plenty of friends here."

I finally gathered my wits and tried to respond: "But Mom, how could I be here to help when I live in Wisconsin? It's not as though I live here and could have helped, but didn't. No. I live a thousand miles away!"

"Jane, I don't want to argue. Dad earned the money. He had the right to give it to whomever he pleased. Plus, he certainly didn't want Dave to get it."

I had hoped that by having this meeting and addressing the subject of Dad's Will that Mom would repudiate it, but I was dead wrong. There was no suggestion of that. I looked at Kathryn. She was looking down at her hands or the table, not at me. There was no help there. Bob was just an observer of a very painful moment.

There was no arguing that point. Dad did earn the money and yes, he had a right. That was the end of the conversation.

What made the will all the more searing was that my father signed it in June of '91 only 6 months after I had confided to him and Mom that retaliation against my feminist activism had had a profoundly negative effect on my previously successful business.

Our financial planner had advised us to list all our present and future assets and liabilities as best we could determine them in order for him to offer us advice on how to weather our economic hard times. During the consultation, Dave informed the financial advisor that Kathryn had once blurted in the midst of an argument that she expected my parents would not divide their estate equally between us. I had put no stock in that utterance, thinking that she was just angry at that moment and was mistaken. Since our advisor's recommendations would hinge on projected assets, including expected inheritances, the planner strongly recommended I clarify what my parents intended.

Following his advice, when my parents visited Wisconsin for Thanksgiving 1990, I took them out to lunch the next day in order to discuss the matter privately—without Dave and the girls in earshot. We went to an old, downtown Madison, railway station that had recently been converted into a popular, yuppie eatery. I was nervous to discuss money with them. They were of the old school. Money matters were private, *nobody else's business, thank you.*

We ordered our food, engaged in small talk about the renovation of the railway station and when there was a lull in the conversation, I broached the subject:

"Mom, Dad, I have something important I need to discuss with you."

The ceiling of this old railway station was very high so the clatter of plates and the chatter of the diners mixed to create a reverberating din. I felt as if I had to shout to be heard—shout about private matters.

My parents heard me though. They became serious and attentive as if to minimize the need for me to shout. I began:

"You know that I've told you that I've made a number of powerful enemies in my efforts to address the discrimination issue in the village and the country club?"

They nodded in a way that seemed wary to me. I continued:

"Well, all of this has had a negative impact on my business."

Mom began to look down at her hands, fiddling with her rings. Dad was intense, serious and seemed suspicious. I felt their ambivalence toward my circumstances. On the one hand, I felt they wished me well, but on the other, their attitude was simple: actions have consequences and they disagreed with my actions.

I continued, but I was increasingly uncomfortable. I was raising two subjects I knew were taboo: feminism and money. I had a close relationship with my parents but there were grounds rules. I was about to break two of them.

"To deal with the economic impact of the backlash against me, Dave and I have consulted a financial planner who says it's important for him to know what kind of inheritance we can expect from our respective families. This information will impact his advice to us."

Barely turning their heads, Mom and Dad looked sideways at one and other, then back to me.

I continued: "Kathryn once mentioned that you may not be including us equally in your wills. Is this true?"

The atmosphere was charged. Neither said a word for what seemed like an eternity.

My mother bit the inside of her lip the way she often did when she disapproved of something. Dad took a deep breath, his eyes scanning from side to side and then to the ceiling. The din roared around us, but there was utter silence and stillness at our table. Even though I had never asked my parents for anything as an adult, even though when I went to college I got scholarships, signed loans and worked in factories every summer to earn my spending money, I felt like a gold digger asking them about their wills. I felt they thought I was crass and materialistic. We were missing each other.

Dad broke the silence. He didn't answer the question I had posed. All he said was: "You don't have to worry, Janie. I will take care of you."

Again, I felt the ambivalence—and the charged atmosphere. He was fatherly, yes, but I felt there was an edge to his assurance.

In the end he "took care of me" all right. I was crushed by his will.

*

The will and mom's attitude towards me sent me into a depression. I had been eschewed by my neighbors and figuratively banished from my birth family. I felt as if I was in a pitch-black room searching for a way out. I imagined myself with my hands flat against the room's walls moving slowly up and down around the space feeling for a latch, a doorknob, a window, a light switch—anything—to help me escape the darkness and the loneliness. Often when I was alone in the car or the shower, an uncontrollable, involuntary wail burst from me. *"Whyyyyyyyyy, Dad? Whyyyyyy didn't you at least tell me before you died? How could you do such a thing to me, take away my childhood homes and then leave for all eternity without saying a thing?"*

It wasn't the money, per se. Dad had, in fact, divided the cash that he had, a substantial amount, between me and Kathryn equally, but it was the banishment that I felt implied in the allocation to my sister alone of the two homes where we grew up. I felt he was rewarding my sister and mother for their lack of conceit—for their humility, for their loyalty, I guess. As Kathryn had once said to me: "You've done whatever you damn-well pleased, Jane."

Now I was paying the price.

204

CHAPTER 22

Dear Mom and Kathryn,

Last month when we met with Bob I had hoped that you both would repudiate Dad's will. Sadly, that didn't happen. Instead you, Mom, approved Dad's disposition of the family homes solely to Kathryn—and you, Kathryn, did not object.

I think I've always been a loving member of our family, a daughter and sister you could be proud of, but it never occurred to me that I would have to earn my inheritance by staying in the area in order to be helpful. I assumed my birth into our family guaranteed me an equal share of the familial assets, especially our homes. Evidently not.

I have come to the conclusion that since neither of you are treating me like family, I will no longer labor under the delusion that I am. It is with a very heavy heart that I say that until and unless this situation changes, I will not be visiting either of you anymore.

Jane

I used to have faith that even though friendships had failed to survive my feminist challenge to the male power structure, ultimately, love would conquer all within the family. Despite our differences, my family had always seemed so solid, so dependable. Mom, Dad, Kathryn and I—even though we hadn't lived together for more than twenty-five years, were still a family unit, a permanent constellation, in my mind. There were four of us in it. Kathryn's marriage, my marriage, hadn't altered that fact. Our family relationship had evolved, of course, but it still existed for God's sake, didn't it? No matter what, our family of four was a unit, the McCalls. I knew my parents and I had disagreed on issues, but what about love? In the end, even if I didn't believe that my father was my superior anymore, he was still my father. I still loved him.

The will was a bombshell. It had shattered my trust in the reliability of anything or anyone. *Nothing* was secure or even remotely predictable now. I had become suspicious of everything and everyone—even my husband of 25 years. If Dad could dispossess me of my childhood homes without so much as a word of warning, anything could happen.

*

A year after sending the letter, I had no communication with either Kathryn or Mom for the first time in my 45 years of life. It was a terrible time. Invariably, each day was punctuated by thoughts of Mom, by the painful realization that I might never see her or my sister again. Every holiday, every birthday, I felt the vacuum and the intense desire to reconcile at any cost. I kept hoping that my mother or my sister would write or call to say that they had reconsidered, that they deemed the will a terrible mistake, so our relationship could be healed. But that didn't happen.

I wanted to capitulate in order to reestablish contact with my family, but I couldn't. Even when my Aunt May, Mom's sister, suggested that I "rise above it," I couldn't. I tried to persuade myself that the will favoring my sister didn't have to bother me; that ultimately, it was a petty issue, material goods, but for me they symbolized much more. Through them I felt my father chastising me and embracing Kathryn because I wouldn't remain his little girl for life.

I perceived Mom and Kathryn's silence and inaction as their agreement with my father's condemnation of me. If I capitulated I would be concurring with the decision that I deserved rebuke. The adult in me rejected that. To continue a relationship with my mother and my sister without their open repudiation of the will, I would have to pretend all the time. I would have to pretend that I was not angry with them for siding with my father or that I agreed with Dad's treatment of me. Maybe another person could do this, but I was not capable of suppressing my intense sadness and anger. I had spent a lot of years trying to find me, trying to value me. I couldn't now repudiate myself. For me it was better to grieve the loss of my mother and my sister than to lose myself.

Or was it?

That was the dilemma: my principles versus my relationship with others, myself versus my loved ones. There's a quotation on my dresser that Dave gave me during my self-exile. It's from western novelist, Louis L'Amour's THE LONESOME GODS. It expresses the intensity of the conflict I felt—and still feel:

"It is all very well to say that man is only a casual whim in a mindless universe, that he, too, will pass. We understand that, but disregard it, as we must. Man to himself is the All, the sum and the total. However much he may seem a fragment, a chance object, a bit of flotsam on the waves of time, he is to himself the beginning and the end. And this is just. This is how it must be for him to survive. Man must deal with himself. It is his reality he must face each morning when he rises."

I knew that life is short, that I shouldn't get hung up on "petty" issues, but this didn't feel petty to me. It involved my self-respect; it involved my reality, the one I had to "face each morning." It involved my freedom to grow, to be an independent thinker and still be a loving and loved member of my family. So I stood my ground with profound sadness and with an acute awareness that as I did so, I missed what I most wanted—a loving relationship with my mother and my only sibling.

During this time my Auntie May and Uncle Warren were my comfort. I was in constant contact with them. Through them I got news of my family.

It was a sunny day in the spring of 1994 when the phone rang in my Madison, WI home. I answered unsuspecting. It was my Aunt calling from Cambridge.

"Janie, it's Auntie May."

"Hey Auntie, what's up?!" I asked, glad to hear from her.

There was a pause before she spoke: "...Jane, I have some bad news."

Her announcement took a split second to sink in. I was unprepared for it, just happy to hear from family, but once I registered her warning every fiber of my body tensed. *Is my worst nightmare about to occur? Has Mom suddenly died...or my sister?!*

"Oh, what?! What's happened?"

"Jane, you've wondered about your mother's behavior, about her attitude toward you, about her lack of engagement in your father's illness, about what seems to you to be uncharacteristic behavior for her. Well, Kathryn took her to McLean Hospital, that psychiatric facility in Watertown. Jane, she has been diagnosed with Alzheimer's...."

There was a part of me that said *YES! That explains everything!* Then, there was the realization: *Mom is dying....*

"Oh! No, Auntie, NO!" As the horror of her words hit, I broke down in tears. I couldn't speak for the sobs....

"I know, Janie, it's awful. It's not fair."

When I was a kid, I had always felt my mother was physically weak. She had had some health problems then. An over-active thyroid had caused her to lose weight and experience shortness of breath when she'd walk up the hill to my elementary school with me. When that would happen I would be terrified that she was going to die right then and there or maybe that night.

But she weathered that period. After a hysterectomy in 1960 she never again seemed ill. I had grown accustomed to her robust health. But now she was facing terminal illness. My decision to stonewall her was premised on a healthy mother. Refusing to communicate with her now was useless—any hope that my silence would cause her to reconsider and renounce the will was gone. She was incapable of such a decision. Now, I simply wanted to salvage whatever relationship I could while she was still able to respond.

I called her immediately.

The voice on the other end of the line was distant, vulnerable and somehow sounded young, innocent, almost childlike. When I identified myself, she was immediately happy. "Jaaaanie! I'm so glad to hear from you." God, I immediately felt terrible guilt. *She does still love me. I still love her. How did we become so estranged? And now she is sick, dying.*

"Mom..." *How can I say this? How can I tell her that I am calling because I know her life, her lucidity, is almost over?* I pressed forward, hoping the right words would come. "Mom, I'm calling because I just learned of your illness. Auntie May told me that you have Alzheimer's. Mom, I'm so sad..." I was choking back the tears, trying to speak and relate over the phone.

I didn't have to be eloquent. Mom was a mother: "It's O.K. Janie. I'm all right. I feel fine...I just have trouble remembering things. There's nothing we can do about it. I just have to keep on..."

In her own way Mom was a heroine. For all her inflating of my father, for all her statements that she was weak and needed support from him, she was very brave as she faced that terrifying confusion. She was assuring me that she was all right....She had always admired the stoic dignity of the Boston Kennedy's in their pain—the only thing that she, as a staunch Protestant and Republican, did admire about those Catholic Democrats! She exhibited the same, herself.

"Mom, you know that the reason that I haven't been in touch is that I've been upset about the will. I still am, but I am your daughter. You are sick and I want to help in any way that I can. Would you like me to come to visit you?"

"Oh yes! Come! Can you come today?" Her Alzheimer's was speaking.

"Not today, Mom, no, but I will be there soon though. I love you, Mom."

"I love you, too, Jane." Her Alzheimer's was not speaking.

*

I kept in close touch with her until she died three years later in May of '97 of a massive stroke. I felt blessed that I had those moments and the meeting on the bus with her shortly before her unexpected death. It was a culmination of the reconciliation and a sweet farewell.

CHAPTER 23

Kathryn was a different story. She had the mental ability to repudiate the will, but hadn't. Instead, in 1995, two years after Dad's death and my self-exile, with Mom's acuity and cognitive function declining, she had my mother sign "quit claim" deeds giving her sole and exclusive ownership of both of our family homes as both Dad's and Mom's wills had stipulated. She then gave Mom a life estate in the properties. Having Mom divest herself of her actual ownership before death was legally advisable to protect the equity from being exhausted if she needed long-term care.

After Mom's burial, when Dave and I went to Manomet, I was not only mourning my mother's death, I was mourning the loss of Manomet and what appeared to be the permanent loss of my sister. I was certain we would never again see one another even though growing up we had been as close and compatible as two sisters three years apart can be.

As a child Kathryn had been the funny little kid with huge, gentle, brown eyes, spindly legs and cowlicks in her shiny, dark hair. She had an endearing innocence and vulnerability about her. The younger sister, she loved to play any game with me: I would wait until she had a box of candy. Then I'd say: "Kathryn, you want to play "doctor/patient"? Invariably, she'd be enthusiastic. I'd say: "I'll be the patient; you can be the doctor, O.K.?" I knew she'd fall for the authoritarian role.

"Kathryn, I'm sick, so you'll have to give me some pills. Do you have any?" She'd think about that. Then the light would go on. She'd reach into her pocket and proudly produce the candies.

"Yep, I've got the pills right here!"

When we got older we laughed about those days.

Now, she had the candy again. But this time she was keeping it all for herself. Dad decreed it. Whether she was an active participant or a passive instrument of his will, the result was the same.

As I walked the beaches of Manomet after our mother's funeral, my eye settled on the foam left by the surf on the wet sand as the waves receded. It reminded me of all the days we had played so happily on that very beach together as children. We had always reveled in collecting the foam in our hands. It had a delicate, silky feel to it. We had sunbathed, played tag and collected clay from the cliffs bordering the beach to make ashtrays. We'd add water to the clay, form it into objects with our hands, let the works of art dry in the sun and then take them home to paint primitive designs on them. The ashtrays proudly presented to our parents had long since broken or dissolved in dishwater. Now the foam and clay seemed emblematic of the evanescence of everything. Nothing was left of what had once seemed a strong and loving family—nothing except death, betrayal and disillusionment.

That my relationship with Kathryn had been destroyed by Dad's will was beyond depressing. I was bitter, pained and had become suspicious even of her. If she really thought, "Dad made a terrible mistake," as she had said when I asked her to repudiate it, why didn't she rectify it? *Or is it possible that she had egged my father along?* As I had told her, she was the only one with the power to fix things. Only she could go to an attorney to have a document drafted for us both to sign so that at Mom's death when she inherited the homes per the will, she would make us joint owners. If Dad put her in a terrible position, why didn't she remove herself from it?

She critiqued, but never disobeyed his will. It seemed that that was never going to happen. Kathryn wouldn't go against my father's will.

She had always been a good daughter in the traditional sense. She never contested what I felt was the gratuitous glorification of Dad simply because he was the male. As such she did all the daughterly duties. She did all the work; lived up to all the daughterly expectations. She didn't seem to feel the tension, the fraudulence of male supremacy that I did. Then again, Kathryn wasn't raised to be the "exception." She was raised to be the norm, to know her subordinate place and accept it. She would never have presumed to judge herself Dad's equal—or even Mom's for that matter. She always remained a daughter in good standing.

As Dad's cancer progressed, weakening him, Kathryn was there to help. She often accompanied him to the chemotherapy, the hospital and doctors' appointments. After he died, she tended lovingly to my mother eventually taking her into her home when Mom couldn't live alone any more. She was the one to hold mom's hand as mom took her last breath.

She did everything a good daughter should.

Because I lived in Wisconsin, I didn't have the daily duties associated with sick parents. Further, because I had been estranged from Kathryn by my father's will, I didn't assist in all of the work involved with the family estate. When Mom died I had refused to pretend for the sake of appearances that everything was fine between Kathryn and me. The thought of standing in a receiving line with a sister who, at the least, was condoning Dad's will, was repugnant. I avoided the scene by not attending Mom's wake at all. After her funeral I returned to Wisconsin with a feeling of profound loss, certain that my relationship with my sister was over; certain that my father's will was being implemented to the letter. The cleaning out of the family homes, readying them for sale, taking care of the paperwork, all of that, fell to Kathryn. If she needed any more justification than Dad's decree to keep the estate for herself, I had surely provided it with my anger toward her once I learned of the will and that she didn't counter it.

*

The envelope had an officious look to it. The letterhead a series of names. The postmark, Boston, Massachusetts. It was from Kathryn's attorney.

Enclosed was a check for one half of the estate proceeds.

213

After all the anger and despair I felt about our relationship in the four years since my father's will had come to light, after my spiteful, paranoid, suspicious treatment of her, Kathryn had ultimately responded with love. She had done what I did not do. By not immediately putting the properties in both our names when Mom signed the quitclaim deeds over to her, she threaded a fine needle. She allowed Dad to do his thing momentarily, perhaps to chastise me even from the grave. But in the end she hadn't allowed the will to impose a life sentence on me.

That she felt the need to follow his will at all was agonizing for me because by that point I had no faith in anything or anyone. I assumed she was going to accept his will for the rest of our lives. That act would have been a symbolic approval of what I perceived as unjustified condemnation and banishment by my father. That would have made our sisterly relationship impossible.

Still, instead of perceiving the will as inappropriate backlash against a daughter who demanded equality as an adult, she saw it as a mistake made by a good man who was hurt and became angry at his daughter: I hadn't put him up in our house when Margaret was an infant; he wouldn't let me have his houses. The source of that anger and hurt didn't interest her. She had no appreciation that it might reflect his sense that a father's will should always prevail. Her desire to execute Dad's will as he wrote it, her unwillingness to reject it despite its treatment of me, proceeded simply from her personal love and traditional reverence for him as her father. While Dad was alive, Kathryn remained the eternal daughter and did not go against him. As such she preserved her affectionate relationship with my parents until the end.

When I suggested to her that by sharing the estate with me she went against my father's will, she disagreed: "No, Jane, I don't see it that way. I didn't go against Dad's will. I did what he directed in it. I inherited the houses exactly according to his wishes. Once that occurred, they were mine to do with as I pleased. I sold them and gave fifty percent of the

214

proceeds to you because you are my sister."

After his death, one of Dad's closest friends counseled Kathryn not to go against her father's will by sharing the estate 50/50 with me. The friend felt that if my father had wanted her to share the houses, he would have put that in his will. Instead he had wanted Kathryn to have both family homes. By that time, however, Kathryn had read Dad's will in a more loving way: he had wanted her to have the properties, period. She *had* done his will. Now she used her power to be a true sister to me.

By sharing with me the reward for eternal daughterhood, she negated the cost of my presumption. In a sense, by disarming the bomb of the will, Kathryn took the hit. Since there is no precedent for the prodigal daughter being rewarded for her independence, I struggle with guilt about the outcome. We took different courses. Kathryn's was completely dutiful, but she never took the payment for that.

In the end when I thanked her for sharing with me, Kathryn said: "Jane, I really believe this is what Dad would have wanted to happen. Dad did wrong, but I think he is happy about this outcome."

She decided that Dad would have wanted me, his daughter, to have half the estate, so she gave me that.

There is part of me that feels the same way, the part of me that knows that Dad did love me...and that I loved him. In fact, I sometimes wonder: *was I stuck in my own head—seeing his will as retribution because of the guilt that I felt for my actions?* Kathryn recently told me that as she and Mom left my father lying in his hospital bed one evening, he called her back and reached for her hand. Weakly, he asked: "Kathryn, you love your mother, don't you?" "Of course, I love Mom, Dad." Reassured, he smiled and relaxed into the bed. She kissed him and left. He died that night.

Did Dad "inherit" Kathryn, so she would take care of Mom? Was he paying her to be Mom's caretaker and because she had been his? Maybe he wasn't punishing me at all for my rejection of him as patriarch, instead only wanting to make sure that Mom was cared for by Kathryn? Was that the explanation for his will favoring her? Or, maybe it was a combination of retribution, anger at my independence, gratitude to Kathryn for her kindness to him, and love for my mother.

I guess I will never know for sure.

I do know that to hold fast to my independence has meant sacrificing the warmth of my parents' love. The choice has been made more painful—and yet more necessary—in the face of mortality: more painful because death deprived me of the opportunity to enjoy reconciliation with him; more necessary because mortality makes the time to become who I am so finite.

I also know that my sister, Kathryn, has eased the pain. We call each other regularly now. We reminisce about the happy times in our childhood. We grieve our parents' passing together. I am grateful for her embrace of me in the face of my father's will. When she says, again and again: "No, Jane, I didn't go against Dad's Will." I am overcome by comfort, joy, and redemption.

*

Dear Kathryn,

On Friday I received the letter and check from your attorney for 50% of the estate proceeds.

Thank you.

For the last 4 years I have felt estranged and insulted. Sharing our family's estate equally with me was an embrace I really appreciate, Kathryn. I have sorely missed our relationship.

We don't always see eye to eye, but we share the bond of blood and more important of happy memories: of warm times in Manomet (I still can't believe it is gone), of the many hours riding in the back seat of the car, bickering and belting out "The

Valleys are so thick with corn that they laugh and sing," of the cherished stops at that ice cream stand on the "old route" home, of Sunday night Denver omelets from chef Dad, of displaying our theatrical talents in the living room at Newland Road with a spirited rendition of "Love and Marriage"—complete with fireplace poker as cane.

No one else can laugh and cry with me, Kathryn, at the memory of Mom lovingly removing the living room curtains at Manomet each September, meticulously washing, ironing and folding them for storage and then reinstalling them the next summer with the solemnity and care of a priest(ess!) administering a sacrament.

When I thought that you were going to ratify the Will by accepting it, I grieved that the kid sister I fondly remembered, the one with the big, round, innocent brown eyes, the unruly dark hair and spindly little legs—my dear sister—was lost to me. She isn't. She has grown up to become a courageous, generous, beautiful and admirable woman—my sister.

Love, Jane

EPILOGUE

I am 72 years old now. The feminist battles are behind me. My parents are both dead.

I am facing the last years of my own life. When I started this book, it was simply a purgation, a way of dealing with the pain of my father's will, with my difficulty liberating myself from eternal daughterhood within and outside my family and with the stress of my quest for political, social and professional equality. I was 47 years old and felt myself rejected by my father and alienated from my community. *What had happened? Why had it happened? How did I get to that place of aloneness?* These were questions that were personal, the answers meant only for my consumption and perhaps for my kids when I am gone.

In the last 25 years I have returned to the book, and to my life in the book, at various times periodically considering publication, mostly at the insistence of Dave and my daughters who want me to tell the story. At first I was reluctant because my mother was still alive. Talking about personal family life, and further, writing about it didn't seem acceptable. Since my mother's death my hesitation has been more complicated. I've had lots of reasons: fear of rejection by agents, publishers, the public; fear that the content, specifically the feminist activism portion, is irrelevant now considering the strides that have been made. At bottom though I think that I have hesitated because in spite of all my efforts to insist on equality, true adulthood, dignity, respect, I still struggle to respect myself enough to think that anyone would want to read what I have written. This book—and my life—present the story of a person whose battles with third parties always became...and still become...battles with *herself*, battles against her own feelings of inferiority.

I can blame that sense of low self-worth on externals: cultural sexism which inculcates all of us women with the knowledge that we are not equal politically, professionally, socially; or on not getting enough unconditional love in our upbringing something most of us experience; or even on Christian religious training that teaches us that we all are the descendants of Eve, but ultimately, whatever the cause, my quest for acceptance as an equal in my relationship with my parents, my husband and my community, has finally been a search for self-love and acceptance.

I call upon the moment when Dave and I were seeing the therapist who forced me to answer the question of how I felt about the length of my parents' stay at our house. I couldn't answer because I had never really contemplated giving much credence to how I felt. I was too busy trying to figure out how my parents and Dave felt and how to satisfy their needs and desires. The therapist used to say: "Give yourself the ticket, Jane." *Give yourself the ticket to ride. Approve of yourself; respect yourself, your thoughts, feelings. Respect others sure, but first respect yourself.* It's not easy. I still don't do it all of the time, but I do some of the time...with effort.

My battles against the Maple Bluff government and the Maple Bluff Club were difficult not only because of their resistance but also because I saw myself through their eyes, not through my own. My difficulty assuming my adulthood with my parents was that subconsciously I continued to see them as my superiors and me as their child. It's difficult to fight something when you don't fully believe it in your gut.

If I hadn't written this book, trying to fathom what happened in my life, I wouldn't have discovered that I, myself, was a sexist. It was only through reflecting on the events and especially on my angst as I stood my ground against sexist treatment, that I realized this. At the time I did, of course, realize that I was having difficulty withstanding the barrage of hostile behavior directed at me, but I didn't recognize that the exact same barrage was coming from within me as well! Even if there had

220

been no third-party resistance to my actions, I would have suffered the same angst because emotionally, internally, I didn't feel worthy of that which I claimed intellectually.

I am always dealing with my sense of unworthiness. I have to battle through it, not unlike the alcoholic with his/her lifetime battle against addiction. Yet as I face the end, when I review my life, I take satisfaction in knowing that in all moments I was courageous and took action. I continue to do this on a daily basis. Now when I look in the mirror, I can be proud because in the face of overwhelming odds, I did not back down. I faced the opposition outside and more importantly within. In the face of fear, I took action.

ABOUT THE AUTHOR

Jane Barry was born in Cambridge, Massachusetts in 1946. While she grew up in a traditional, mid-century household, Jane was part of the wave of women entering the workplace 'en masse' with the feminist movement of the 1970's. Her life has been a search for the liberation, internal as well as professional, that the era promised. Jane lives with her husband of fifty-one years, David, a fellow feminist, and their Sealyham, Badger Boy, on Boston's North Shore.